Find Your Flame
Why Motivation Matters More Than Talent

Find Your Flame
Why Motivation Matters More Than Talent

SOPHIE BENNETT

Photograph by John Cleary

THE CHOIR PRESS

First published in the United Kingdom in 2018 by
The Choir Press

ISBN 978-1-911589-84-6

Advance Praise for Find Your Flame

A game changer for companies looking to build a positive, inclusive culture
Daniel Barnett, employment law barrister, Outer Temple Chambers

This fast-moving, enjoyable book gives you a series of practical ideas and strategies to become a high-energy, motivated person in every area
Brian Tracy, New York Times best selling author

If you want to achieve meaningful results and true success, you're going to need motivation – and lots of it. This book shows you just how simple it can be to discover your unique talents and stay fired up for long enough to make a real impact in the world.
Dorie Clark, author of Entrepreneurial You and Stand Out, and adjunct professor, Duke University Fuqua School of Business

When you read a beautiful little book that absolutely does what it says 'on the tin', you know you've found something you'll treasure. it's superb.
Paul Dunn. Chairman B1G1, Creating a world full of giving

Find Your Flame is a gamechanger for the study of motivation. Why people do or don't do stuff, and with what level of enthusiasm and success has both intrigued and puzzled the biggest brains forever. Sophie Bennett has supplied a valuable and missing piece of the puzzle. I especially love her model of the 5 motivational forces or flames that light the way and get us fired up. The perfect blend of readable examples, stories and science make it a great read for anyone seeking peak performance and fulfilment in life and business.
Rob Brown, Host of the Top 100 Club Podcast, Author of Build Your Reputation and Founder of the BD Academy

Sophie has written a simply stunning book which inspired and challenged me on so many levels. Simply understanding your flame and how to maximise your potential will make a massive difference to your life.
Simon Chaplin – Chairman of Greenstones and founder of Socks Up Simon

No two people are the same. Yet underlying each of us is the set of simple codes that make us who we are. *Find Your Flame* identifies the simple underlying code of motivation. Five elements combine in each of us, in infinite combinations, to motivate us; and to guide us as to how we motivate others. I adore simplicity, particularly when it clarifies complexity. *Find Your Flame* does this brilliantly well. It is an extraordinary work that will change the lives of anyone who reads the book and applies its wisdom.
William Buist, – Strategist, Mentor, Catalyst.

As a motivated entrepreneur and business leader in my younger years I assumed others were motivated in the same way as me. Then later being aware we are all different I have for many years been trying to tap into what "makes them tick" with limited success! However, I believe Sophie's new book will be ground-breaking in helping me and other leaders understand the different ways the people within our businesses and organisations are motivated. Tapping into and learning from what makes others' fired up from the stories within this book is bound to lead us to greater success.
Paul Hargreaves, Chief Executive, Cotswold Fayre Ltd

Most people know what they should do to move their lives on for the better but for some reason never seem to get round to it. In her brilliant book *Find Your Flame* Sophie Bennett solves that exact problem. She puts a metaphorical rocket up your backside to show you what motivation is, how to get it, how to use it and how to keep it – even when you don't feel like it!
Michael Tipper, Author, Speaker & Consultant on Effective Learning, Leadership & Life

Find Your Flame is not 'another book on motivation', nor 'another book for leadership': I am impressed that Sophie Bennett has really cracked a new code for personal leadership, personal motivation that can change cultures of businesses and organisations. A book that I personally will recommend for the leaders I work with as a 'must read'! Thank you, Sophie, for taking the lead to these new insights!
Nienke van Bezooijen: Public speaking expert for speaking authentically with impact, International leadership mentor, International Bestselling Author and Speaker

Sophie Bennett's book *Find Your Flame*, will certainly be on the must-read list in my leadership programs! We all know that motivation is key for becoming successful. Sophie's description of the five motivational forces makes us aware of the possibilities for an individual to identify his own unique triggers and start up and maintain their personal fire!
Henk Bremer. Founder of LDpe (Leadership Development Processes and Enablers) and former Director of Competence and Leadership Development for Capgemini Continental Europe and Asia Pacific

The book I wish I'd written! *Find Your Flame* is the first book I've read in a long time that offers a new take on motivation without getting bogged down in psycho-babble. Lots of useful stories to illustrate and help embed key ideas. Nice one ...
Simon West, Technologist I Strategist I Leader

This amazing book really cracks the motivation code! The book tells you what buttons to push if you want to motivate people. A must read for everyone in HR who wants to fire up their team and give their leaders tools to do the same.
Christian Kromme, Futurist & best selling author

Find Your Flame is not only a very good and easy read but it brings together in a concise and real way the essence of effective and strategic leadership. As Leaders, we all recognise where we are and what we need to do, and I know that many will be able to leverage from Sophie's strategic mindset. This book will add much value to many. Enjoy a memorable read.
Michael Doolin, B.Comm, MBS (HR) FCIPD Managing Director, Clover HR

I think this book nails it. And I don't say that often. A neat combination of stories to lean into (a journey of discovery and the little snapshot case studies) and some rigour behind it (research etc...) makes me want to read more. Short chapters. Not up itself. No feeling of holding back.
Robert Craven, Keynote Speaker, Author – Grow Your Digital Agency. www.robert-craven.com

One of the biggest mistakes a leader can make is to assume that others are motivated by the same things as they are. This book brings this faulty assumption to light and give leaders' the awareness and tools to fire themselves up to fire others up. What a different business environment we would see if this fire were to truly take hold!
Sue Coyne, Best Selling Author of Stop Doing, Start Leading and expert in leadership and motivation.

Motivation matters. It's what helps people advance further and faster in their career and earn more money, be productive, experience more satisfying relationships and be happier than less motivated people. We all have different motivation triggers and our own unique and distinct motivational type. What motivates one person can de-motivate another, but no one motivational type is "better" than another. This book will help you understand the DNA of motivation. The Drives, Needs and Awards that make up your own motivational type. Find Your Flame is a great read – you won't want to put it down!
Eve Grace-Kelly, Success Coach

Sophie is one of the most fired up people I've had the pleasure to meet. In this gem of a book, she synthesizes the best of behavioural psychology and provides the reader with a simple, yet powerful model for personal and professional growth, delivered through a down to earth, relatable tone. If you want to achieve your goals, your way, get this book!
Antoinette Dale Henderson – Keynote Speaker, Executive Coach, Author of Leading with Gravitas and creator of the Gravitas Programme

One word. WOW. This book unlocks a new way of thinking about motivation and brilliant if you want to find out what really makes you tick. It uncovers the secrets to the DNA of motivation, so you can decode what really drives you and influences your success, so you can be a strong leader of your own life, and empower others to be the leader of theirs.
Marie Oakes, Founder of The Trend Academy

The ability to express complicated ideas and concepts in simple terms demonstrates mastery and Sophie has done that with this book. She explains in simple terms how to tap into your natural motivation in a way that I haven't seen expressed before. It's a brilliant handbook for helping you find your personal route to achieving your goals

Dave Clark – Lead Consultant at cs4b, CEO of Benemen UK, CEO of NRG Business Networks and Managing Partner of DSC Metropolitan LLP.

Best-selling Author Sophie Bennett has done it again! *Find Your Flame* is a little book about Motivation that punches above its weight. Revelations from an in-depth investigation into the mystery around motivation while presenting a new paradigm with examples of where it comes from and how powerfully it works at its best. A compelling read with lessons for how to receive and successfully dispense more of it. Valuable knowledge not only for Leaders but for everyone who is driven to be self-motivated too!

Valerie Dwyer – Entrepreneur, Transformational Success Coach, Mentor, Speaker.

Contents

Foreword

Careers tend to follow a pattern dictated by three questions. At the start of your working life the big question is: *What?* Among all the potential occupations to fill your time what are you best equipped to embrace as your own? What are you actually good at? What do you enjoy doing?

And so, you try numerous alternatives. You wait at tables, serve drinks, clean floors, flip burgers, answer phones, dive for pearls, clean out stables and so on. The *what* becomes clearer and, though still fuzzy, becomes ever clearer as your career develops.

And then the big question tends to revolve around: *How?* Jobs in organizations are about *how* to get things done. How do you fit so many tasks into one day? How can you get the job done to the highest quality?

In particular, *how* is the all-embracing theme of any managerial role. Management is the art of how.

And then finally you encounter the biggest question of all: *Why?* Why are you actually doing what you do? Why do you persist in getting out of bed every morning? *Why* is the question which lies at the beating heart of leadership.

Of course, careers are mainly lived in the wrong order. They should start with *why* and then move on from there.

The trouble is that understanding why is actually a lifetime's work. But, the earlier you figure out what turns you on and what excites you, the more likely you are to be engaged in your work and happy in life.

Sounds easy. It is anything but. Understanding your own motivation is demanding and highly personal work, but it holds the key to how we fare in the working world and to our personal happiness.

This is why *Find Your Flame* is an important and useful book. Sophie Bennett understands where the sparks come from and how you can best ignite them to unleash your motivation as well as your talent.

What motivates you is a unique personal journey. You no longer have to travel it alone.

Stuart Crainer

Co-founder Thinkers50

Part 1

The Motivation Mystery

Act as if what you do makes a difference. It does.

William James

Prologue

Igniting The Fire

We all have moments that determine our path in life.

Moments that light a fire inside us and change everything.

They aren't always obvious at the time, but in hindsight, you realise that the little spark of motivation to do something became a life-defining moment for you.

That's what happened to businessman Paul Dunn, the Chairman of B1G1,[1] a global business giving initiative. He's a man on a mission to create a world "full of giving". The B1G1 idea is that you buy one and give one. Everything changed for Paul one day in 2006 on a visit to India. He was attending a program in Bangalore when his friend Alex asked him to go for dinner, and quickly added, "If it's OK with you Paul, I'm going to bring a friend."

Paul and Alex arrived at a restaurant called The Taj. Paul picks up the story, "It was anything but a Taj, this was not 6 star, it was a long, long way from that. There was a guy waiting for us, about 35 years old, dressed in a white shirt." Alex introduced me. "This is pastor Silva".

Paul recalled a moment of utter embarrassment when he asked, "Is that pastor as in P.A.S.T.O.R or is it pasta as in PASTA?" Despite being a moment that he would rather forget, it's a moment that sticks in his memory. He recalled it as if it were yesterday (more about pivotal moments later, you will discover that they have surprising levels of impact on our day to day motivation).

[1.] www.b1g1.com. Paul Dunn has a stunning track record of starting and growing businesses and is a four times TEDx speaker.

So, Alex, Paul, and Pastor Silva went in and sat down for dinner. The Pastor turned out to be quite a storyteller. He wove his tale, "About four years ago I was asked to go and minister a community of four thousand people on a tiny island off the coast of India. Then something happened just over a year ago, close to Christmas time."

Paul visibly shuddered as he remembered that part of the conversation, "I should have realised the importance of the date, but I didn't. I just kept listening".

"I was teaching a class of kids at Sunday School. All of a sudden, we heard a strange noise, unlike anything we'd ever heard. I asked the kids to stay calm while I walked outside. I could see a couple of kilometres away there was a wall of fast-moving water that was clearly going to engulf us all."

The penny dropped. Paul suddenly got what Pastor Silva was talking about. It dawned on him that what he was talking about was the 2004 tsunami.

"I rushed back into the Church and told the kids that we were going to play a game. We were going to all hold hands and run up the hill as fast as we could. We just got above the water and watched as the beautiful little church that we had just been sitting in was crushed like a lunchbox."

And it wasn't just the church, that little group consisting of the Sunday school teacher and a dozen children watched as all the buildings near the church were washed away. Inside those buildings were the parents, families, and friends of those poor children.

Paul now realised why he had been asked to dinner when Pastor Silva told him that he had been the only person left to look after the children. Alone. With no resources. The entire village was gone. He was all they had left.

He was on a mission to get help to raise enough money to feed and educate the little ones. They now had a place to stay, but there were other things that they needed. Apparently, schools in India are free but the uniforms and textbooks aren't, plus the children needed to eat. Paul took action and did what he could on the spot. The Pastor told him how much they needed, Paul thought the number he gave him was for one of the children, but it turned out to be for all the kids. He got his cheque-book out but instinctively knew that that wasn't the end of things; it was likely to be just the beginning ...

"A few weeks later I got an email and inside was a photograph of the house where the kids were living. It was just a one-room house, very sparse but there were the children, sitting in a circle with food in front of them. In the next photo, the kids were sitting with books and study-ing them, but it was the 4th photo that hit me. There was a close-up shot of the outside of the house. Over the door was a sign saying **The Paul Dunn Home**. That hit me. I had made a difference in a way I had never done before."

Paul was at pains to say it wasn't the recognition of his name being over the door that hit him, instead it was the realisation that he had made an impact that had changed the lives of those kids. Giving had just become immensely personal. It wasn't about the money. It was about the meaning. There was no escaping the difference he could make after that. He couldn't just open his chequebook again and forget about it. Those days were over. Life would never be the same. It had become his responsibility at that moment to step up and appre-ciate the potential for impact that he had. Potential that he couldn't leave to someone else. It had his name on it – literally Paul had found his flame.

It had never happened to him before in that way. He had been shifted from being fired up by one primary thing (he had always been in busi-ness, and had a track record of getting great results and had become famous for it in IT and then accountancy circles), and now he was on fire about something else. That sign over the door would lead to a series of events that would create more giving impacts than he could have ever imagined; over 138 million by early 2018. More about what followed from that (and what we can all learn from Paul's journey) later. For now, what's important about that story is that we all have moments in our lives that make us who we are. Moments of joy, absorp-tion, connection, winning, deep emotion or revelation. In their recent book *The Power of Moments*[2], Chip and Dan Heath,[3] recognise and decode the power of moments in our lives and demonstrate that one defining moment has the potential to change the course of our entire lives. What *this* book is all about is how those moments shape our lives, light up our internal flame and how we can engineer moments and circumstances that keep us ignited and effortlessly motivated over the longer term.

There is a lot of talk about talent; hiring talent, discovering talent, developing talent and nurturing talent, but what does that really mean? The road to success is littered with 'talented' people who didn't make the cut. Talent is no guarantee of success; it's simply a starting point. It doesn't matter how talented someone is if they don't have the drive to do the work and overcome the inevitable host of obstacles that are guaranteed to get in the way.

As you read through this book, hear some of the inspiring stories and insights featured, you won't hear much talk of talent. Most of the people in here started doing things because the actions they took (however hard they were to do) gave them huge payback and sowed the seeds of a new set of habits that led to success in their chosen field. Those feelings were slightly different for everyone, but they all delivered something positive such as self-worth, being in the zone, being part of a group that they liked, getting respect from someone that mattered to them or something equally powerful. Very few of them started as a great 'talent'. In fact, for many of them there were other people who were much more talented than they were, yet they were the ones who reached the top. They were driven, they cared, and they felt that what they were doing mattered. They found their flame. I hope you will find yours too (and if you already know what yours is, I hope to get to ignite it more often).

When there is a burning desire inside of you, you don't need to be

---

[2.]   *The Power of Moments* is published by Penguin Random House.
[3.]   Chip Heath is a senior professor at Stanford Graduate School of Business and Dan Heath is a senior fellow at Duke University's CASE Centre.

externally motivated do you? It's when you *aren't* following your true path that you need to 'motivate' yourself, or when you *are* doing what you love but the world outside isn't helping you; that's when you need drive. But underneath all that, if you are on the right path for the right reasons, you will find the flames you need deep inside yourself. When the right flames ignite in the right order and everything aligns, that's when your so called 'talents' come to life. I believe that 'talent' is largely about what you have the passion and drive to spend your time and energy mastering.

It's a nice thought to want to feel inspired most of the time, but that's not how it works. Inspiration is often something we only realise we had in hindsight. But there are sparks of something great burning inside us all the time, even if we are too busy to notice them. Sometimes these sparks are negative feelings that we work hard to escape from (we'll talk more about that later). Sometimes the sparks are those 'feel good' moments that fuel us to achieve amazing things. What's more surprising is that to some level, we spend our entire lives looking for and repeating one or a combination of the feelings that set us on a particular path in the first place. They run like a golden thread throughout our lives, and they often end up driving almost everything we do.

It also gives a structure for motivation and drive that's not quite like anything that's been studied in this way before. That's because much of the work around motivation has looked at the evolution of our motivations over the course of our lives, rather than the early sources of motivation that leave deep impressions on us that often impact our choices for life. The deep-seated triggers that we will explore together in this book don't work like that. They aren't gradual in their development; they are often instant. They hit you like a bolt from the blue.

By understanding what lies behind the triggers of motivation in our daily lives and the pivotal moments that precede them (because there's always a story behind the story) you will start to see just how important they are. It is even possible to engineer motivational trigger moments more often for yourself and for others. You can only do that when you understand the driving forces that set them off. When you can do that we can change the future for your team members, your company, and yourself.

Those triggers and pivotal moments can inspire us to move forward and help us to keep going when things get tough. Motivation plays a massive role in resilience. After all, if you aren't motivated to reach a goal, have a good feeling or achieve something specific, what's the point in being resilient? You might as well give up, sit at home, and watch daytime TV. Motivation and resilience are close brothers from the same stable.

By discovering more about triggers and pivotal moments you can set up the conditions for more of them in your own life. Motivation leads to action, and action leads to success.

When you know the DNA of motivation, and you can do the same for your family, your team, and your company, you can influence how much more fired up they are than ever before. Now that's something worth knowing about. That's what this book is all about, helping you to dive into the five elements that motivate us, so you have the tools to live life in a way that inspires you.

Just five elements might not sound much, but they come together in an infinite number of ways. What's really exciting is to know that as your understanding of motivation gets deeper, you will perform better yourself and get better at motivating, leading and inspiring others too. I wrote this book to help as many leaders and future leaders to become more effective and as successful as possible without adding a great deal more effort into the process. That might sound counterintuitive, but in motivational terms, it's an important distinction. That's because it's often the case that *stopping* doing things is often even more effective than doing *more*. That can make motivating others really simple sometimes. Just do less, yet get more.

It's often much easier to **remove** things that **block** motivation than it is to do a host of extra things to increase motivation.

Sometimes we just need to get out of the way. Sometimes we just need to get out of our *own* way too.

You are going to discover what specific mistakes many of us unwittingly make that can accidentally demotivate other people, and bring those (often sub-conscious) actions into your awareness. You are going to gain new skills to manage yourself better, lead others more skilfully and become more successful in just about every aspect of your life by the time you get to the end of this book.

In short, you will probably become a more successful person and become a better leader. You are going to discover what it was about Paul Dunn's experience that made it so powerful and how you can tap into that same chemistry whenever you need it – without having to go to India to find it.

Sophie Bennett – 2018

Chapter 1

The Golden Thread

Being fired up is the energy and fire that lies behind every success, and yet we know so little about what it is. The Cambridge English Dictionary gives two definitions of motivation:

- The enthusiasm for doing something, and
- The need or reason for doing something

That might tell us what it is but doesn't move us any closer to the big questions about how we get more of it when we need it.

One of the most respected researchers in the field, Dr Edward L. Deci, Professor of psychology at the University of Rochester and director of its human motivation program says in his book* that, "self-motivation, rather than external motivation, is at the heart of creativity, responsibility, healthy behaviour, and lasting change."

If that's the case, and I believe it is, it turns out that intrinsic motivation is an important thing for all of us. I also believe (having studied so many motivated people) that, ironically, it is something you need to cultivate. Even intrinsic motivation doesn't last, and it's how we manage our thoughts and emotions, how we set goals, plan and measure our progress that becomes the difference that makes the difference.

The challenge is that we are all motivated by a slightly different set of factors, and I set out to discover what they were.

The key to motivation has always been a holy grail of leadership. Organisations want to motivate their team members to be fully engaged in their work. Businesses need to motivate their customers to buy their

---

Why We Do What We Do, Edward L.Deci with Richard Flaste by Penguin 1996.

products and services (and be demotivated to buy from their competitors!), and not for profits and NGO's want motivated donors, staff, and volunteers. So, trying to find a single cause of motivation is always going to be a tall order.

There's no doubt, whether we like it or not, we do live in a world where those who can motivate themselves go further than those who can't; and those who can motivate others as well go even further.

The energy of self-motivation applied day in and day out eventually attracts other motivated people. Motivated people get noticed by other motivated people, and they get ahead. They have an inner fire that helps them to succeed. As Sir Ken Robinson said[4], being in your element gives you energy: not being in it takes it from you. I believe that being *in your element* is the key to high performance. That is something that you can create, cultivate, and manage. When we do that we can all become superstar self-leaders and magnify our influence with others.

The speaker and author of the recent best-selling book **Influence –** *How to Raise Your Profile, Manage Your Reputation and Get Noticed*, Warren Cass, reminded me recently that passion and motivation aren't much help without the self-discipline to take action. Unfortunately for most of us, those two things don't always appear at the same time (wouldn't it be great if they did!). Sometimes we are on fire and compelled to take action, and sometimes we have to drive ourselves to get things done. It's just a fact of life. We oscillate between the two states. You will discover more about that when I share the *Motivation Wave* with you in a later chapter. Talent only takes you part of the way. Without the drive to stick out the tough times you will get stuck on the side-lines wondering what happened.

Success isn't an accident. Short-term success might appear random, yet it's anything but. It belongs to the motivated. As I ran through the hundreds of hours of interviews that I've conducted as part of this research, the piles of white-papers, stacks of books, post-it notes, and

---

4. *Finding Your Element* by Sir Ken Robinson PhD and Lou Aronica. Published in the UK by Penguin 2013

articles on the subject of motivation, I suddenly realised that there was a problem with my approach. I was looking for something so variable and based on ideas that originated with Ivan Maslow way back in the 1940's. It was great work, and Maslow kept developing his ideas, but even though human nature hasn't changed a great deal since then, the world we live in has changed – dramatically.

A useful formula for motivation has so far been elusive and that's because motivation is just one word, yet it means many different things to different people. It's not a fixed state.

For a route to motivation to become useful, we need to define what it means to each of us and see if there is a pattern that helps us re-create it at will. If we can do that we stand a chance to work out how we can put that knowledge to use in our lives and workplaces.

Even the word 'motivation' is the start of the issue. That's because it's most often used as if motivation was a noun – *a thing*. There's the first part of the problem – it's not *a thing!*

It's an idea, a feeling, and a response; and it's **different for everyone.** There's a whole ton of variables. You start to see the challenge ahead. No wonder we have had a problem finding a formula for it!

Motivation is much more than a word or a formula; it's a feeling that moves us. Sometimes it has a bigger purpose behind it; sometimes it doesn't. Sometimes it is a strong and powerful feeling that drives us; sometimes we are just a little bit motivated.

You might be motivated to get yourself a sandwich, but that's not going to help you conquer Everest or win the Olympics.

Motivation is a moving target, and it changes from one hour to the next. It's also heavily dependent on context and your environment. It can be balanced out by rewards for taking action (carrot), or the losses or punishments for not taking action (stick), following from the carrot and stick approach that's been well documented elsewhere. We'll think more about that later in the book because it's vital we understand the impact of using both strategies on ourselves and with others.

Motivation is complicated because it's not one thing. We all have different factors driving us. Even if we are passionate about the same cause or purpose, we all have a different way of going about fulfilling it. Motivation is complicated, yet we need a way to decode it if we are going to influence ourselves and persuade others that life can be better if they motivate themselves too.

But I had a feeling that there was a golden thread there somewhere and I was determined to find it. There had to be a pattern in all those papers, books and interviews. There had to be a key to starting the engine of peak performance.

Chapter 2

The DNA of Motivation

The DNA of Motivation Revealed

As I suspected, there was a pattern – and it turned out to be surprisingly simple. It turned out that what motivates us falls into five distinct areas. These are five different feelings we are looking for, and when we find them, we are compelled to experience them as often as possible and with as much intensity as possible. Humans are motivated to seek out and then repeat one or more of these five types of experiences because they feel good.

Each of us has all of the drivers in different amounts and in a slightly different order of importance. It turns out that there's a code. Think of it like a motivational DNA that's simple, elegant yet infinitely diverse. It's a code that expresses itself without your conscious intervention most of the time, even though I acknowledge that there will be times when you need to find motivation from nowhere so you can get stuff done and we will get to that. There are some things that we are motivated to do *without* thinking about it much – if at all. We find some things effortless to get started, and then the power of momentum takes care of the rest. That's what the code is about, understanding **effort-free motivation**, and what gets in the way of it.

The DNA inside your body is made up of just a handful of simple elements[5], yet despite that tiny number of building blocks, an infinite

---

[5]. DNA is made up of backbone called a nucleotides based on a phosphate molecule and a sugar molecule and 4 different bases that make up our unique code: The bases are adenine (A), guanine (G), cytosine (C) and thymine (T). It's the specific order of A, G, C and T within a DNA molecule that is unique to you. Those handful of molecules are enough to creative all the diversity of life on our planet. Incredible.

variety of possible combinations are responsible for the massive diversity of life we see on our planet. We share 60% of our genes with the humble banana and fruit flies, and 96% of our DNA with chimpanzees. All that diversity from just five building blocks! Well, we shouldn't be surprised that our motivations are just as diverse, and like DNA, there is a code.

I believe that the discovery of these five different types of motivation will unlock breakthroughs for individuals, for teams, and for organisations.

Here are the five motivational forces that are The Five Flames of Motivation. So named because they light us up and fire us up to succeed in our work and our lives.

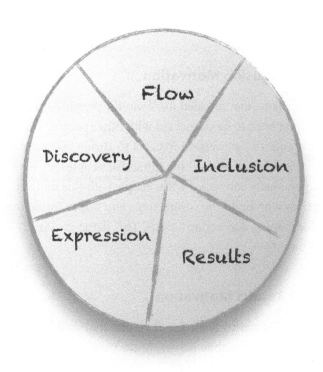

Flame 1 – Flow Motivation

The first flame is the feeling of being lost in things. This drive shows up strongly with sports people (especially coaches and non-competitive athletes), some academics, in jobs where deep concentration is essential (such as software designers) and in some entrepreneurs. People who are flow motivated talk about being 'transported' by what they do. They enjoy times of intense concentration or absorption when the rest of the world falls away, and everything plays out effortlessly. It's an intense feeling that's inwardly focused and deeply personal. They talk of being *In The Zone*. It's most often experienced during activities that involve developing a level of mastery. It's about being in the moment and about the **process** itself rather than the **outcome**, which is an added bonus. This flame is called FLOW motivation.

Flame 2 – Inclusion Motivation

The second flame that revealed itself was the people flame, and it relates to our strong need to be connected with other people. This is the social motivator and it's a powerful force. It's so strong that people with high levels of this drive do astonishing things for people they have never met or even personally connected with. People with this motivational flame are the ones who build the connections and bonds inside our communities, companies, and organisations. This flame is called INCLUSION motivation.

Flame 3 – Results Motivation

Winning is a powerful feeling and results motivation is all about the competitive element that drives some people to do extraordinary things. People who have high levels of this drive are much less concerned about the process of how it's done than people who are motivated by flow. They are much less affected about the *quality* of the experience. They care far more about the **result**. The involvement of other people only matters if it affects the results. This drive is all about the scores on the doors. Whether it's an Olympic medal or a record-breaking sales quarter, this group of people are fired up by measurable achievement. This flame is called RESULTS motivation.

Flame 4 – Expression Motivation

Then there are the artisans. These are people who care deeply about the human condition and the emotional side of life – even if they don't show it readily. They often find a way to express their identity and passion through some sort of artistic outlet. They may act, speak, paint, write, dance, compose, play music or design beautiful things. You will often find them at home in the creative industries, in medicine, developing soft skills or in the human resources department of a business. They are at home with the arts, and often their hobbies are in one or more of those areas too. This group make all our lives richer by connecting us to who we are as human beings. This flame is called EXPRESSION motivation.

Flame 5 – Discovery Motivation

A high level of intellectual curiosity defines the fifth flame. The people with strong motivation in this area talk about a burning curiosity to know more, understand more, and find out what makes things tick. It's the drive that fuels new innovation and discoveries. People with this drive are, for example, behind the exploration of deep space and want to find out where we came from and how everything works. It's the motivational engine behind most scientific, medical, and physiological discoveries. As well as academics, world-class coaches in every area from sport to business have it too. This flame is called DISCOVERY motivation.

The Motivation Performance Engine Revealed

Wow, there it was. When I realised there were just five key elements all sorts of patterns started to appear. Many things that at first seemed complex suddenly became simple. I called the five elements the *Five Flames of Motivation* because they shine a light on what drives so much of our behaviour and our decision-making. I quickly started to realise that these flames don't just light up individuals – they have a collective power too. They light up teams, projects, companies, movements, and even entire countries. We will explore collective motivation later in the book. If you have an interest in company culture, it's something that's going to be really helpful to you.

So how do the flames work? Well, it seems that for all of us (and almost every social structure that is human-made, including businesses) we have one very dominant flame, one bright secondary flame and a smattering of the other three in varying proportions.

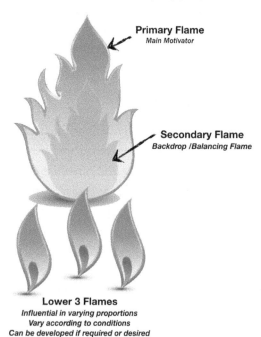

Primary Flame
Main Motivator

Secondary Flame
Backdrop /Balancing Flame

Lower 3 Flames
Influential in varying proportions
Vary according to conditions
Can be developed if required or desired

What Is "The Fire"?

Motivation is essential to achieve anything useful and productive over a long period of time. Without it, you just can't sustain the effort, and it's almost impossible to stay engaged with what you're doing for long enough to succeed. It's not surprising that employee engagement is so high on the list for companies to improve; yet despite the focus on engagement, the numbers are dreadful. According to a 2017 Employee Engagement report by Aon[6] Hewitt's Global Culture and Engagement Practice who collected data from over 1000 organisations, just 25% of the global workforce rate themselves as 'highly engaged', and in both North America and Europe, the overall trend is that engagement is on the slide even further. There is a pressing need to have new ways of looking at what *really* motivates us and to apply the research to the places where we work.

There is something exciting about highly motivated people.

Fired up people have a passion and drive that seen from the outside appears to be inexhaustible. They are the people who make things happen and achieve amazing things. They also help other people realise their potential. They are the movers, the shakers, the influencers, and the people who seem to attract all the luck.

We all know someone like that, and we all want to be more like them (even if we don't admit it, and our desire for extraordinary success is our little secret.) We don't all need to be famous, wealthy or well known to enjoy success and happiness. Some of the most motivated people I researched and interviewed are tucked away doing great things in our communities, in our schools, in our companies, charities, and families.

Fired up people are everywhere. Yet when we want to be motivated ourselves on demand or to light up other people, the flames can be really difficult to access. When we try to force it, we often find hesita-

---

[6.] http://www.aon.com/unitedkingdom/attachments/trp/2017-Trends-in-Global-Employee-Engagement.pdf

tion, doubt and procrastination. We step back from the edge of greatness and retreat back into the safety of our comfort zone.

It's clear that fired up people do things very differently; it's not that they are on fire every moment of every day about everything that they do (nice thought, but totally unrealistic). Instead, they have different strategies to keep the fire burning.

I figured if you wanted to know how to stay motivated and achieve things that most people wouldn't even attempt, the best people to ask were the driven people who have motivation and energy to spare.

For too long I believe we have been asking the wrong questions about motivation, especially in business. We have been asking 'How do we motivate people? How do we keep our employees engaged? What if we were to ask instead, "What if we look beyond the task itself and find out what really motivates us to do great work?" and "What might we be doing to dent peoples motivation by accident?"

I went on a mission to ask the most motivated people I know (and some I didn't know yet) how they get motivated and stay motivated and how they still achieve great things even when their motivation wanes.

So that's what I did, and it turns out that it's all pretty simple stuff. There are clues everywhere from the people I interviewed and the survey I set up to capture as much data as possible. Clues in their language, how they focus on things, and interact with people, and even in their hobbies. You just need to know what to look for. You don't need a 27-page psychometric test to do it. I've got nothing against those tests by the way. In fact, much of the research for this book is based on the work by social scientists and psychologists that produce those very tests. I just question how useful they are on a day-to-day and minute-by-minute basis. The reports usually get locked away in a draw, or the data has to be limited to a few people because of ever stronger regulations about data protection, but great things about The Five Flames idea is that we always have our eyes and ears with us. They are the only tools we need to recognise and implement the ideas in this book. We just need some simple tools to filter what we see, hear, and feel so we can use what we know.

That's what the fired up philosophy is all about: Simplicity.

So, what ignites those peak performers?

And how do they keep the flames alight when the going gets tough? Let's find out.

Everyone Has the Flame Inside

I believe that we all start out with enough fire in our belly to last a lifetime. Yet somewhere along the line much of it gets lost in the grind and responsibilities of daily life. We start off as kids full of playfulness and enthusiasm. We don't begin life with a critical mind, full of self-consciousness and wondering if we are good enough. That comes later. As we grow up, people throw cold water on our ideas and expect us to conform. I'm going to be referring to the things and people who (often accidentally) demotivate us as Extinguishers.

We get the spark of an idea, then the monumental effort that it's going to require to bring it to life can be enough to put us off taking action. But some people have found a way around that. I call these people Fire-starters. These are people who have found a way to stay fired up despite the self-doubt and detractors out there. Fire-starters have enough motivation to achieve incredible things.

What's different about that small percentage of people who have the resilience to stay motivated however difficult the game of life gets? What's fundamentally different about:

- People who use hardship to achieve more
- People who are driven by the desire to be part of something bigger than themselves
- People who use their energy to create extraordinary results
- People who move us emotionally through their music, art and poetry and,
- People whose unstoppable curiosity is the force behind the discoveries that change the world

What if we were able to understand what drives those people? How much could we learn that we could apply to our own lives and workplaces? A great deal it turns out. So, let's see what we can all learn from the Fire-starters and what we can avoid doing to ourselves and others from the Extinguishers.

Chapter 3

The Future Belongs to the Motivated

Motivation in a Fast-Changing World

The world of work is changing at an exponential rate. Although for a long time it has been cheaper to move information than it has been to move people, our workplaces have been slow to catch up. We still travel to work and sit in offices all over the world. We still have managers controlling much of our daily work. We have lived and worked in a command and control type management structure for so long (since the Industrial Revolution at least) that it has become the norm for most people to rely on others to tell them what to do. Huge numbers of people don't have to think too hard during their daily work.

Yet we are moving from knowledge workers to decision workers. That's some of the hardest work there is. Humans aren't always brilliant at making decisions; unless we are powerfully motivated. So, motivation has never been more important. Many of the jobs that can be done without much thought aren't going to be done by humans, motivated or otherwise, in the very near future. Your own role might be at risk from the robots, or your team might be worried about their future. Either way, there's a whole lot of change that's scaring people.

It's not always easy to stay positive in a time of such rapid change, and our world has never seen such a fast pace of change. There have been some big political upheavals too: Europe and Brexit and the election of Donald Trump in the United States have all created huge uncertainty for people.

The landscape has changed in the last few years with the increasing adoption of robotics, artificial intelligence, drones, machine learning, and automation. As a result, there has been a cataclysmic shift in the way that we work, and the changes are only just getting going. I believe that shift that we have seen in the last decade is only the start. Governments are struggling to keep up with the changing needs of companies, workers, and international trade and most of us struggle to see around the next bend as things move faster and faster. Bosses are battling to keep up with managing millennials, and everyone is struggling to see where things are going next. It's not an easy time inside corporations, and they need help to stay positive and bring what we know about motivation into the workplace.

People who rely on others for motivation are going to find themselves in an increasingly precarious state. They are going to struggle to survive. Many people have become so reliant on other people telling them what to do that they are at a loss when there isn't someone to direct them. For those people, it's not always their fault; it's not just laziness. It's simply a reaction to their situation at home when they were young, at school, or in their early days at work. If you were in a position where thinking for yourself got you in trouble, you would likely stop doing it!

Not thinking and not self-directing is often a reaction to getting negative feedback or to poor treatment for making your own decisions. People don't always make the right call, and the culture of organisations often means that there is something to be gained by pointing the finger at people to deflect attention when things go wrong.

That's a motivational killer.

The culture and environment we work in has a significant influence over how we feel. When we get clear about the simple things we can do to make other people feel better, it's amazing just what can be done and what can be overcome.

The future belongs to people who have the motivation, ambition, and capacity to reinvent themselves and the role they play in the world.

The future belongs to people who are prepared to educate themselves and become more flexible, adaptable, and self-directed.

The future belongs to the Fire-starters.

More and more people are choosing self-employment, or being forced into it through redundancy, because of company mergers or a simple change to the nature of their work. A lack of job security is driving a whole further tranche of people to set up on their own and deal with the rigours of making it all happen without the traditional support network surrounding them. The tail end of the baby boomer generation who are now in their 50s and 60s are far from retiring. Instead, they are starting consultancies, life coaching businesses, and health and well-being companies. They can't afford to retire. Millions of people are following their passion and turning those passions into business to supplement ever diminishing pensions and savings (if they are lucky enough to have any) that offer hardly any returns. As Bob Dylan told us, the times they are a'changin' . . .

The changes aren't slowing down either. They are speeding up.

The trend line for self-employment can be clearly seen in the data from the UK office of National Statistics[7], the statistics may not be bang up to date, but the trend line is clear. Self-employment is rising rapidly.

With all these changes taking place and with the knowledge that it's the driven of this world that get things done, self-motivation is clearly an important quality to have.

We aren't all motivated all the time, even when there are things out there that we really want. When the alarm clock goes off, it's all too easy to hit the snooze button. When you want to lose a few pounds but there's something tasty on the plate in front of you it's easy to think short-term and the result can wait. If we want to overcome those little acts of self-sabotage, the only way to do it is to give ourselves the tools to work around what our brains would have us do naturally, and that's

---

[7.] Source https://www.ons.gov.uk/employmentandlabourmarket/peopleinwork/ employmentandemployeetypes/articles/trendsinselfemploymentintheuk/2001to2015

to take the path of least resistance: Hit that snooze button! Eat that doughnut!

We know it won't make us rich or make us slim to do those things, yet we do those unwanted behaviours over and over again and we end up torturing ourselves mentally.

We shouldn't be so hard on ourselves because we are *designed* to behave like this. It's natures' way of keeping us safe. Evolution has programmed us to conserve our energy (snooze, in case we need to run away from the tiger later today / eat now because it might be the last meal we eat, and we could starve! / don't go the gym, stay on the sofa because we need to preserve our energy in case we need to save ourselves).

So, how do we overcome that?

We're generally much better at taking action when we are moving toward something positive than we are when we are just moving away from pain. Moving towards a positive also has a longer lasting effect on our motivation.

Pain might be a great trigger, but it doesn't have a lasting impact on our willingness to do things for *long enough* to get the success we want. Why is that? Well, when you think about it, nature has programmed us in a way that makes us do *just enough* for the pain to stop, and then get back to our comfortable place again as quickly as possible. Think for a moment about the motivation pattern of a serial dieter (I know what I'm talking about on this one ...).

You start feeling fat, you still eat yummy stuff until you feel bad enough to take action, you take positive steps (morning sit-ups, replace chocolate with fruit, cut the carbs etc., etc.), you start to feel better, and the actions work. The pounds drop off, but you never quite reach your target weight. You slip back into old habits. I have harsh personal experience that feeling bad is only a temporary motivator.

To make change stick, you have to look for the bright spots and magnify them. In their brilliant book *Switch- How to change things when change is hard,* Chip and Dan Heath talk about the power of helping people to find the bright spots and build on them.

One of the 'bright spot' stories in the Heath Brothers book, tells the story of aid workers with a tiny amount of money to work with, finding solutions to childhood malnutrition in Vietnam. The workers could have done lots of scientific research into the causes, attempted local political change or gone down the route of fundraising or education programs, but they didn't have the time or the budget for any of those things.

They wanted to make a difference on the ground as quickly as possible and bypass some of the traditional routes just mentioned. So instead they looked for the bright spots. They went to look for families who were poor but whose kids were well nourished. They didn't look for the problem; they looked for people who had found the solution **for themselves**. Quite simply, they looked for the bright spots and built on those.

Sometimes motivating yourself and others is as simple as focusing on the things that are already working or that make us feel good and leveraging them. Sometimes that's as much about giving people the conditions they need to thrive and letting them get on with it. If we don't give people the right circumstances or the right encouragement, and we get in their way for long enough (even if we don't mean to), people can become so discouraged that they get apathetic and stop trying altogether.

You only need to look at the tragic employee engagement figures in many companies to know that business has a real problem with apathy in our workplaces. The millions of people sitting on sofas struggling with their health and well-being tell you the same story. We need solutions because there's nothing more sapping or more contagious than apathy. Apathy can travel through organisations, families, and communities like wildfire. That's not the sort of fire we want.

It's a tragedy when we have opportunities but don't have the courage or motivation to take advantage of them. That leads to mediocrity. That's rubbish. Seriously. You don't want to end up there. If you do, you are reading the wrong book. We don't do mediocre around here. We do ambitious, challenging, horizon broadening, stretching, successful, satisfying, and visionary things in this book. So, if you are up for that read on.

Maybe you picked up this book because you're looking for ways to motivate yourself or others in your work or home life. Possibly you are one of the rare people that this book sets out to study and learn from and you and I just haven't connected yet. Or maybe you are super driven but struggle to manage yourself effectively from time to time?

The Future Belongs to The Fire-starters

Whether you are interested in motivation from a personal point of view or from an organisational one, there is no doubt that our world is changing at an exponential rate.

You might be asking yourself what all this has to do with being fired up. Well, it is clear that the trend is towards more and more people demanding more choice about how they spend their time and earn their money. People want more control over their lives. That means there is ever more need for self-leadership, self-direction, and account-ability. None of those things are easy, so it's vital to be able to access an inner force that keeps you going.

We all have the power to become a catalyst for change. That can only happen if you have the ability to manage your own motivation. If you want to lead others, then you are going to need to understand what motivates *them* so you can **make things happen** by leveraging the power of others. Either way, or both ways, you are going to need to become a catalyst for sparking activity.

Your own success, where you work, who you interact with will largely depend on your level of self-motivation.

Just look at the increasing numbers of self-employed workers.

Quarter 1 (Jan to Mar) 1993 to Quarter 1 (Jan to Mar) 2016

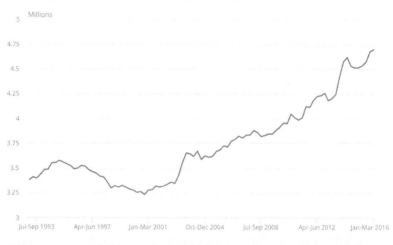

Source: Office for National Statistics, Labour Force Survey

Figure 1: Number of self-employed workers

The people that the graph represents, are a self-employed army of consultants and freelancers (and those who aspire to be one of them), are your potential customers too. It's vital to be able to have more than one way of building up a type of profile of their needs, desires, and drivers. It's just not enough to appeal to demographics anymore. We need to understand what drives people's decision making.

We are moving away from demographic profiling, towards what marketers call psychographic profiling[8]. That's a whole new area. Marketing expert Barnaby Wynter describes psychographic profiling as being "not a description of who the target market is but how they feel; what's worrying them and what they are hoping to do about it; where they are looking for the answers and why, how they can improve their quality of life."

---

[8]   Read more about practical psychographic profiling in *The Brand Bucket - make your marketing work*, by Barnaby Wynter.

What Barnaby is talking about is understanding what *really* motivates people. This book isn't about marketing. However there's no doubt that great marketing is rooted in the understanding of human motivation. Building a useful and simple motivational profile will help you to do that.

A good motivational profile should be able to help you to know yourself better, to influence others more powerfully and to give you the power to shape your own future. Increasingly that's going to mean taking more and more control over our working lives. To be able to influence and lead others you absolutely must be able to read what motivates their behaviour.

Being The Boss of Your Own Life

More and more of us want to be our own boss. Dutch entrepreneur and futurologist Christian Kromme has a chapter in his recent book *Humanification*,[9] called The Rise and Rise of the Entrepreneur. He points towards a strong trend of independent entrepreneurship and voluntary collaboration with others and that we are moving to a world where more and more of us are driven by purpose and less by money. One day it's possible that we will have a Universal Basic Income where we are only going to do things that inspire us. Christian believes that time is not as far away as many of us think it is.

We all have to become more and more self-motivated and self-directed. People working for companies are also expected to be better at managing themselves, in part because our bosses are no longer watching our every move or even working in the same locations as we are. When you put all that together, it becomes clear that there is going to be nobody telling this vast army of new entrepreneurs, self-directed workers and growing body of self-employed people what to do. We

---

[9.] *Humanification* by Christian Kromme published by The Choir Press. Note of a personal interest here because Christian is a client who I helped to develop the stories for his book. The core ideas are all his and he's a captivating thinker.

need to have the motivation to find out for ourselves, and the energy to implement what we learn.

The days of being micromanaged are coming to an end. Each and every one of us need to take increasing amounts of responsibility for our own results and our own passions and projects. There is a massive growth of industry in providing specialist knowledge online to allow people to create businesses on a shoestring by using tools available in the cloud. Every small business can now position itself as a media company with the ability to outrank fortune 500 companies online just by using some clever and original marketing ideas delivered for free to millions of people via viral videos on platforms like YouTube or Facebook – or platforms that haven't even been invented yet.

This alone has totally changed the landscape for companies of all shapes and sizes and it has made self-employment and entrepreneurship a real possibility for millions of people who could never have dreamed about that level of freedom before.

There is a downside though. Once the initial excitement of the freedom that entrepreneurship and self-employment gives us has worn off, a new reality takes its place. The new reality is that isolation can sap motivation; induce bone crushing self-doubt and loneliness. The same applies to employees who are remote workers functioning for long periods isolated at home. There is also the potential of becoming culturally detached from your fellow workers and the vision of the company.

Over the years I've done a lot of coaching and consulting for businesses, large and small, and mentored many self-employed people who thought that life was going be much easier than it turned out to be.

The pattern is often that they start off with an idea followed quickly by the reality that it's not as easy to make money as they expected and motivation wanes quickly. Suddenly, for the first time, there is no boss or leader to help repair the motivational carnage inflicted when something goes wrong. Resilience is tested and only those with the right self-management tools are able to make a success of it. Motivation, drive and energy are everything. Whatever you care to call it, we have a responsibility to nurture it in ourselves and develop it in others who are seeking it.

I decided to come at this project by starting with the most motivated people I could find and ask them questions about their motivation. I thought it would be useful to know things like;

- where they thought their fire came from
- how they manage it well enough, and for long enough, to reap the rewards of success
- What was happening underneath the subject matter;

Let me explain that last point. When we look at people who are successful in any field, it's entirely natural to look at the subject matter. For example, when you see a great academic who specialises in fossils, you might assume that the passion is fossils – but when you understand the 5 flames of motivation, you quickly realise that there is a more significant force in play than the fossils themselves.

I have attempted to look beyond WHAT ignites these people and endeavoured to find out WHY it ignites them. When you understand the forces at work, the content suddenly is less relevant. You start to really see what the drivers are. Content is often just a red herring. When you get the 5 Flames, you will know exactly what I mean.

Meet The Fire-Starters

A collection of inspiring people kindly agreed to be interviewed for this book. From a multimillionaire entrepreneurs to best selling business authors, respected speakers, a futurologist, a jungle trekking medical doctor, an award-winning dyslexic young entrepreneur, a veteran Irish record-breaking triathlete with a seven-figure business, a Business School leadership expert who has worked with hundreds (if not thousands) of businesses. There is a marathon running vet, a military pilot (who tells a remarkable story of what motivated him in the darkest of moments) and a leading research scientist in one of the world's most prestigious institutions. Every person was chosen because they have shown exceptional drive and personal motivation.

There is much you can learn about yourself from these remarkable people, and there are probably some tools, strategies and ideas that you can put to use straight away. There will be other things that you will mull over and maybe come back to when the time is right. One of the fascinating things about many of these people is that they don't think they are remarkable, at all but each experienced moments of impact that have had a lifelong effect and led them to achieve extraordinary things because they were motivated to take the next step, and the next and then the next. Their moments of impact were often so small that they were invisible to anyone but themselves, yet they changed lives.

For one person it was his treasuring a few felt tip pens and colouring book when he was a little boy. For another, it was listening to a Pink Floyd as a young teenager. For another, it was a single sentence from a teacher who will probably never know the effect she had, and one person was even inspired to go into business, so he could eat as many puddings as he wanted. These moments weren't always spectacular from the outside (in fact they would have almost certainly been missed by anyone but the individual concerned) yet those moments changed lives. They changed the lives of the people who experienced them, and the ripple effect has since affected the lives of millions of others.

These revelations will let us into a private world that few of the participants have ever opened up to people about before now. It's a rare chance to use their stories to trace the roots of some of *your* passions and to re-evaluate the effect of the earlier experiences, giving you the opportunity to build on them or re-engineer your behaviours and reactions to things (especially things you aren't happy with). It's not just about looking backwards either, it's also about gaining more capacity to notice the motivational triggers of others so you can ignite other people, get more done with less conscious effort, and to become a better leader yourself.

Chapter 4

Discover Your Unique Triggers

If you can find your unique trigger, you can fire it up anytime you want.

One great example is Robert Craven, an international keynote speaker, business coach[10] with a blue-chip client list. His Directors Centre business has advised hundreds of businesses, and he has written more than 10 books on business strategy. He has an ability to manage himself and think clearly under pressure that has created a worldwide demand for his company's services. He's a leaders' leader. He is truly at home on stage.

Speakers are an interesting example of being fired up because they can't *wait* for a moment of motivation to hit them. Speakers have to be fired up on demand at the exact moment they walk on stage. They also need enough energy and stage presence to bring the audience along with them. That's not easy in a big auditorium when the energy is low. When they manage it, as Robert always does, it can be transformational for everyone in the room.

There are some useful lessons that speakers can teach us all about peak performance moments because for them it **can't** happen by chance, it **has** to happen by design. When we did the interview for this book, Robert had just returned to the UK from New York where he had to be on fire for an audience of over 900 of Google's leading global partners at the biggest Google conference of the year. He was the last

---

10. www.directorscentre.com

speaker on the final day; not an easy slot to fill. You know you are going on stage and facing an exhausted crowd, full to the brim with new information, tired and probably eager to get home. I asked Robert how he managed himself so that he was on fire at the right time to deliver a great performance.

"You have to know how to wind yourself up and manage your nerves so when you hit the stage, you are at the very peak – with enough coffee, enough adrenaline, and enough knowledge."

He described the complex relationship between speaker and audience, which is no different to a manager or leader trying to influence other people's behaviour in any situation. "It's about managing yourself well enough to manage them."

Wise words indeed, as it turns out that many of the most successful leaders have the most emotional control. By that I don't mean they are cauldrons of emotional suppression, it's that successful people are able to choose how they feel by reasoning through what's the most useful way to feel and respond at any given moment.

Do you react or respond? Are you able to get fired up on demand like Robert Craven? Do you have enough fire to be able to influence the energy and minds of the people listening to you?

If you want to be successful, or engage and inspire other people, then you have to be able to motivate yourself enough that they want to have some of your drive.

I have often noticed that it's energy that people really want. If people want information they can get that anywhere; we all have Google in our pocket these days. But Google is no substitute for human energy.

You have to be able to generate enthusiasm when you need it because it's the basis of your personal effectiveness, your ability to lead and your ability to create your own success. So where does it all start?

How Early Experiences Impact our Motivation

Our early experiences can be very revealing about what is going to fire us up later in life. When I asked networking and business growth expert Rob Brown if he remembered a precise moment when he realised he was more motivated than most, he was unequivocal. "The other kids didn't really focus. They just messed about. I can remember, about the age of nine or ten being in the corner of a room where I'd made a little den in my house. I'd been given some felt tips for Christmas; it was that pack of 30 felt tips. I had all the different colours, and it was wonderful. I'm not an artistic person, but I got those pens and a colouring book. I would be very diligent about colouring in all of these things making sure all the colours are right and not going over the lines, making sure the felt tip lines were all going on the same way. Moving the colours around, so I didn't waste the ink in one felt tip, so they'd last as long as possible. I'd be sitting there for hours. Even back then I remember thinking – where does that come from?"

Even back at that early age, Rob was reflective of the fact he was making the most of things. He's now a professional speaker and is an expert in the mechanics of business growth, and no detail escapes him. It's no surprise that he works with a lot of accountants who love the detail and his ability to zoom out and see the big picture. For the early part of his career, Rob was a teacher. That experience gave him insight into motivation and how we are affected by our environment. His believes that school can make or break drive and he has seen that from both sides: pupil and teacher. "It's a system that forces you to conform." Not great if you are moving into the businesses of tomorrow where diversity of thinking is what's needed, not a new generation of people who can only follow orders. In my day-to-day business, I provide leadership consulting, and I've noticed just how many companies unwittingly fall into that same trap. They expect people to conform, rather than unlocking their potential.

These early lessons learned from observing kids, taught Rob Brown some lessons that he still values today. Like many people who help others succeed, he is dedicated to lifelong learning, and he showed his commitment to mastery that day with those felt tip pens. The clue that he was going to be driven to excel was right there.

There is no single magic button that you can just press to get fired up every single day. If only. But there actually IS a combination lock. There are several combinations, and each of us has a slightly different one.

Have you ever met someone who you have referred to as having a 'burning ambition'? Now you know what it means. It's a flame that can't be extinguished. The people who we admire often defy convention. They push themselves harder than most, adapt to change, take on seemingly impossible challenges and overcome obstacles that most sane people wouldn't even consider taking on. They are the change makers, the Olympians, the millionaires, the Oscar-winning actors, the leading professors, the social entrepreneurs, and the business leaders.

If you are a leader already, this book is going to help you to identify the people who have the capacity to drive through change and innovation in your company. You will be able to instantly recognise the community builders, the potential sales stars and the brand ambassadors who will help to build loyalty and connection with your brand and they might be tucked away in corners of your company where you might not have thought to look before. You are also going to find simple ways to help them deliver their best work and be fired up by doing it. You'll get clues and ideas about how and what to identify in your best people to give them what they need to stay with you. In today's fast-moving job market and access to new opportunities on every smartphone, it's becoming a massive challenge to attract and retain the best people.

According to research[11] 48% of people said that they would take a pay cut if they could change their manager! That figure demonstrates the need for good management and great leadership. By the way, as

---

[11.] https://happymanifesto.com/2017/12/02/dear-ceo-let-people-choose-managers/

fashionable as it is to interchange the terms management and leader-ship they are not the same thing. A great leader can inspire people, build a great vision and set out the strategy, they won't necessarily have the same skills as a great manager who can organise things, manage people, deal with complexity and set clear boundaries. I believe that many managers don't get given sufficient training to carry out the day-to-day tasks of a manager with skill and confidence. Management is often a messy business with conflicting priorities: reporting the numbers and managing people with emotions and complicated lives and coaching people to develop their skills without micro-managing them. That's a tough ask, and they usually still have to do the day job at the same time!

There are a host of competing priorities at the middle management level that put managers under high levels of stress that they very often leak onto their team. Motivated leaders can provide fuel for motivated managers who in turn can motivate their teams – but only if they can communicate with them in a way that they understand. That's not always easy, because we are not all the same.

Fired Up or Driven (and Living Life Above The Line)

I'm sure you know from experience, that you can't stay fired up all the time. It's just not realistic, and even if you could, you would burn out pretty fast. So, a great deal of what you need to stay in any game long enough to be successful, is to be able to manage your own motivation. Because you can feel on fire one day and be utterly lacking any motiva-tion the next. But the work still needs to be done, doesn't it? So, we all need to find ways to manage ourselves and help others to do the same.

Look at the picture below. The wiggly line represents our motivation. It goes up and it goes down. It doesn't stay at one level for long. It's always on the move. The top of the peaks represents our positive moti-vation; the times when we are fired up about something. The troughs are the times when we don't feel like doing what we need to do, and at that point, we have a choice. We either bump around on the bottom of the trough for a while, or we drive ourselves until we are back on the up again. Most people who don't actively manage their own motivation spend most of their lives living on the line through the middle of the wave. Not driven, not fired up, just steadily travelling through time and ambling from one day to the next. What's important to understand is that the extremes are natural. Go with the flow and ride the peaks for as long as you can when they come. Surround yourself with people who peak more than they trough. Their energy will rub off on you and you, in turn, will have a positive effect on others. Eventually, you can spend most of your life above the line.

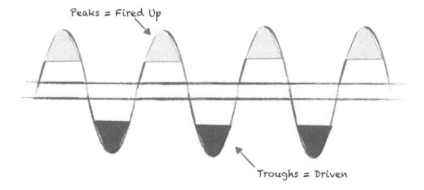

Being professional is doing things that you love to do on the days when you don't feel like doing them
Julius Irving – (Retired American basketball player)

A great example of managing your own motivation came from an interview with marketing and strategy consultant and New York Times bestselling author Dorie Clark[12]. Dorie teaches for Duke University's Fuqua School of Business, HEC-Paris and IE Business School in Madrid (two of Europe's leading business schools), and has lectured extensively

---

[12.] Dorie's best-selling trilogy includes *Reinventing You, Stand Out* and *Entrepreneurial You* and has over 400 free articles on her website www.dorieclark.com

in Europe, Asia, and North America and blogs regularly for the Harvard Business Review, Entrepreneur, TIME, and other major publications. She was also one cool dude to interview and a fascinating person. Dorie is one highly motivated human, and it was fascinating to hear her take on personal motivation.

"Anything feels less fun when you *have* to do it. The way I try to guard against that is to use my effective procrastination strategy." What a great idea! "I procrastinate doing something I *have* to do by doing something else that I will have to do *eventually*, but I don't need to do now. It feels more fun to do it now, instead of the other thing I have to do. Let's say I have committed to write an article for you, and I told you I was going to get to you by close of business on Friday, and I know I should do it because it's due soon. But instead, to warm myself up, because I absolutely don't feel like writing this article for you, instead I'll write an article that is due to somebody else next month it just feels more fun and more creative. That's because the deadline is further out and I'm choosing to do it. So, by being aware of that, I try to get ahead of the curve and do the work as far ahead as I can. Then it still feels like a choice and feels like fun."

Dorie knows that Flow doesn't come easily when you're under pressure to produce results on somebody else's timescale, so instead of battling with that, she has invented a very creative and fun way to manage it. It's a great example of self-knowledge leading to discipline that in turn leads self-leadership and results in success. Dorie knows what motivates and what de-motivates her and she uses that to do great work in her own time.

The better you get to know yourself, and which bits to learn to change and which bits to keep just as they are, the more successful you will become. Success is a process, not an event, and it's rooted in self-knowledge.

Fired Up Mentors

If you want to absorb some of the energy of a highly fired up person, then the good news is that they often make very enthusiastic mentors. Just make sure that you have the energy to move at speed and the mental agility to keep up with them. They will want to challenge your mental acuity and test your stamina at every opportunity.

One fired up person I know is a Fellow of the entrepreneur charity, The Princes Trust[13] and has mentored over 5,000 potential and fledgeling entrepreneurs. He prefers to stay under the radar, and although we had many conversations about this book, he preferred to stay that way. He is over 75 years old and complains daily of how slow everyone else seems to be. That's a typical frustration I have heard over and over again as I listened to the stories and experiences of highly motivated, driven people. Mr Princes Trust is physically fit, trim and in better physical shape than many 30-year-olds I know. In fact, despite a very demanding life indeed, has managed to stay in clothes the same size since his 20's. Although his priorities in business have shifted from his own success (he has everything he needs) he has transferred his drive to help other people do the same. His drive has not diminished; it's merely shifted focus a little and expanded well beyond himself.

Moving From Stick To Carrot

American author Daniel Pink wrote a great book called *Drive; the Surprising Truth about What Really Motivates Us.*[14] Pink is a former Whitehouse speechwriter for the former US Vice President Al Gore. That alone tells you that he is clearly driven himself, you don't get into the Whitehouse by sitting on the side-lines waiting to be asked.

[13.] A UK charity founded by the Prince of Wales to help disadvantaged and inexperienced young people to go into business

[14.] First published in Great Britain in 2010 by Canongate Books Ltd and by Riverhead Books in the USA.

Pink's exploration of drive was an interesting and useful piece of work because he was actually comparing what elements incentivised and motivated people and what switched them off. It was a book clearly written for businesses to help them understand that many of the reward and compensation schemes designed by companies go against what people really need to be motivated. His point was quite clear; that our understanding of psychology, how we pay people and how we treat them and manage them at work is at odds with the science. What we know and what businesses do are poles apart. It's an argument that he makes effectively.

Pink looked in detail at what motivates people at work. He looked at the difference between extrinsic motivation (carrot and stick methods of getting people to do what you want them to do – something he terms Motivation 2.0) and the more positive intrinsic motivation (which he calls Motivation 3.0). Pink concluded that there were three primary things at work that can motivate or demotivate people and he found that there's a gap between old-fashioned rewards and incentives and recognising what people really need. Here's a quick summary of the main points that Pink uncovers. The three core elements of his motivation 3.0 are Mastery, Autonomy and Purpose.

Let's look at those things one at a time. First of all, take mastery. That does apply to certain jobs, but not every job. You could hardly get fully absorbed stacking shelves in a supermarket. Mastery doesn't have much payback there. Not every job can involve mastery, but most can induce Flow if you have the opportunity to get into a rhythm and focus in a certain way. We will get the triggers for flow shortly because although there's a relationship with Pink's mastery; they aren't the same thing.

The second element of Motivation 3.0 Pink refers to as Autonomy. He defines that as having a level of self-direction over four things:

- Their task
- Their time
- Their team and,
- Their Technique

Of course, people like to manage their own time, but not everyone has the skills to be efficient when working autonomously. To some people, it's just downright lonely, or it's more responsibility that they want to take. There are large numbers of people who don't have a choice over the tasks they have to do, and some people have terrible time management skills. I heard one UK Public Sector HR manager ask if the drive towards autonomy at work would become a 'piss-takers charter'! It's a good question because giving groups of people autonomy takes a great deal of planning and the whole business strategy needs to be aligned with it. I agree that nobody likes to be ordered around without any care or consideration, but I don't hear about people who wake up in the morning with their mind on getting more autonomy, they just want to get through the day as pleasantly as possible and come home without being stressed out to the eyeballs. I believe that we can aim higher than that.

If we know what fires people up, we have the opportunity to really engage them. As we go through the motivational flames, I think you will start to build a bank of ideas about how you can do that for the different profiles of people.

Those who seek high levels of autonomy often choose self-employment or entrepreneurship. Just reducing the temptation for managers and team leaders to micromanage others can be enough to give many people all the independence that they need to be happy at work.

Finally, Pink talks about people needing a sense of purpose. Yes, I agree that we need to know there is a point to what we are doing but for many people, the main point is to earn money to pay the bills. Purpose is a luxury for many people, and we shouldn't forget that.

The flames of motivation go deeper than any particular job itself. For me, the science might be on Pink's side, but the practicalities of putting his findings into action are more challenging. That's because his triad of mastery, autonomy and purpose are very abstract ideas. People aren't always aware that these things even exist at work and don't get up in the morning chasing them. I can't remember the last time my husband leapt out of bed on a quest for mastery, or I was driven to write a proposal out of a sense of purpose. (I deliver on my promises – the sense of purpose is very much behind the big ideas for the business, but the tasks themselves are driven by other factors like the expectations of others, commercial necessity, professionalism and honour). Mastery and purpose conversations don't tend to happen around the water cooler and in tactical project meetings – and yet that's where a great deal of motivation and de-motivation happens.

I believe we need something more concrete to work with that people can directly relate to. The idea behind this book was to create a simple framework that would do precisely that and to identify simple things that people could put into action that would fire them up about what needs to be done and help them to stop unwittingly pouring cold water on the intrinsic motivations of others.

If we recognise the feelings people are looking for (and we all prioritise different ones in different proportions), I believe business managers and leaders have the power to make work more engaging and much more fun. Carrots all round!

But sticks haven't entirely gone out of fashion yet as evidenced by British Member of Parliament Gavin Williamson who said in a recent speech[15] "I don't very much believe in the stick, but it's amazing what can be achieved with a sharpened carrot . . ."

What does that show us? That motivation is still in the dark ages in some areas and politics is definitely one of those areas; whichever country you happen to live in. I believe that these archaic attitudes towards consensus and inclusion are one of the reasons why politicians are struggling to engage younger people who place higher values on inclusion. Politics happens on the shop floors, management meetings and boardrooms of many companies and the manoeuvring that occurs there is just as destructive. Political activities inside a company are a sure-fire way to damage trust and reduce inclusion. It's a cancer on a

---

15. Conservative Party Conference, October 4th, 2017.

positive culture – and that pours cold water on all but the most ambitious of people.

There's no doubt that motivating others is an art as well as a science. We will be studying both together throughout this book. One concept I think will help to summarise the actions you can take yourself is the idea of being a motivational martial artist. When you first start most martial arts, you get given the suit to wear for training. Your level of skill is visible by the colour of the belt that you are allowed to wear; white belt for beginner through a succession of colours to a black belt for the most advanced. There are levels of black belt of course – the finer and finer distinctions of skill, self-leadership, and the ability to teach others. For the purposes of this book, we are going to use the white for beginner levels of skill, green for intermediates and black for the most advanced motivators. So, let's move forward to a truly black belt idea.

Chapter 5

The Dynamic Motivation Formula

If there is a single golden thread here that I hope stands out of this book for you, it is that getting, being, and staying fired up is MUCH easier than you think.

When we think about motivation, we often look for more. That's what white belt people do. They add more stuff. They make more lists. They look for more information. But it's not the big stuff that we are missing on a minute-by-minute basis. It's the little things that get in the way that is often the problem.

If you just stop doing a few things you didn't even know you were doing you will be able to make a huge impact. If you manage or lead other people, then just by reducing the unintended motivational knocks you accidentally give them, you will help other people to do their best work. How can we stop giving energy to things that don't support us in achieving things, or don't change the world for the better?

What would your place of work be like (and this even applies if you work alone!) if, instead of frowning and getting frustrated, you just stopped doing that? It sounds a simple enough idea, doesn't it?

It is.

But it's not *easy*.

It's hard to stop putting effort into things that have become habits we aren't even aware of having. Bad moods can be habits. Tight shoulders take effort to produce, but if we don't realise we are doing it, we can't fathom why we end up with a headache. First, you need to become aware of what you are thinking, saying, and displaying and then you need to have enough mental bandwidth to notice the same about other people. It is possible though. It's just a skill. One that we can all develop, with a bit of practice.

It takes 10, 20 or even 100 times the effort to re-light a fire that's gone out. In work done many years ago by a tennis academy, researchers showed that it took around 10,000 repetitions of something new to for a tennis player to be able to do it on autopilot, but it took 40,000 repetitions or more to make a faulty serve and correct it so that the replacement behaviour came naturally. It's much harder for us to correct faulty behaviour (especially if we don't know it's defective!) than it is to do something new.

Instead of adding things in, how much could you take away from what you do to get more success?

Doing the opposite of something less productive or helpful isn't as difficult as you think. If you saw someone scowling when they walked into work each day, the opposite isn't for them to start smiling. That's way too complicated, potentially too big a shift for someone to make on command and wouldn't be consistent with 'how they are when they go to work'. The opposite of scowling would simply be NOT scowling. A neutral expression. Open to whatever the day has to offer.

So, when I talk about doing less of something I really mean it. It's not about changing things radically. I'm talking about just stopping doing things that get in the way. So, what could you take out of your day that would reduce a little of life's friction?

If there would be something that you stopped doing that could reduce friction for someone else, what would that be? That's a question I hope to challenge your thinking with all the way through this book.

In the west, we have had a long-standing set of beliefs that add up to the idea that more equals better. Yet, if we work harder, we don't always take home more money. Sometimes we burn out or damage our relationships instead.

If we train more, we don't always get stronger; sometimes we get injured instead.

If we pay more attention to detail, we don't always end up with perfect results; sometimes we get in more and more of a muddle.

You can see the principle now. And yet even though it makes sense, all around us, there are messages that subtly suggest more is better.

Work harder, and you will achieve more.

Win more, and you will be more popular.

Stress more and people will think that you care more.

Yet many of these connections are false, and won't you get where you want, because they cause you to waste your energy. You will just burn out. Instead, staying on fire about life and work is about focusing on the right things at the right time and being efficient. In other words, doing as much as needs to be done, and no more. Doing more than that is wasteful – and tiring. There is a better way.

Just enough is enough. Instead of more, how about doing less and getting more enjoyment instead.

Peak performance always takes effort, but not necessarily in the way that we first think. Sometimes the effort is learning NOT to do something that gets in our own way. So, here's a question to ponder on when you get a quiet moment. What are you doing unknowingly that might be dampening your spirits or the spirits of those around you? What thoughts do you have that impact on you? What self-criticisms do you dish out onto yourself that make you feel bad or call your talents into question? What could you stop doing that would make you feel better? What behaviours do you exhibit that might make other people feel less energetic or positive when they are around you? And what difference would it make ten years from now if you just stopped doing one of those things?

If you can uncover what you can stop doing so that you are only left with things that propel you (and others) forward faster and with less friction, this book will have made a positive impact. So let's get started. Let's look at the 5 Flames that light us up and check out what we can do less of, so we don't throw water on the fire; our own fire – and if you run or are part of a team, their fire as well.

Less really is more.

So, let's find out how to put that idea into action.

> *People concentrate on doing the right thing, whereas they should concentrate on not doing the wrong thing.*
>
> **FM Alexander**

Part 2
The 5 Flames

Chapter 6

Flow Motivation

6.1 The Flow Flame

The waters around the islands of Fiji are a stunning deep blue. The wind constantly blows in that area of the Pacific making the conditions perfect for sailing. Professional skipper Paul Adamson was responsible for safely moving the 90 ft ocean-going luxury super-yacht called Lush and its passengers. It's one hell of a boat. Hardly surprising when you discover that the boat belongs to former Formula 1 boss and multi-millionaire entrepreneur Eddie Jordan[16]. Paul, Eddie, their spouses, and crew were part way through a round-the-world trip of a lifetime, when Eddie had to go back home to deal with some business, so Paul sent the rest of the crew home for a break. For the next 6 weeks he and his wife had the boat to themselves. Paul picks up the story.

"We were leaving Port Denarau, and I remember standing on the bow of Lush looking out at that beautiful turquoise ocean. I remember feeling the awesome power of the wind and the boat keeled over as the sails captured the power and propelled us outside of the reef and into the blue ocean. It was just an amazing feeling. I felt so grateful that I had the skills to sail this thing and the trust of other people to be able to do it."

Paul was experiencing flow; a culmination of honing skills, being focused, achieving mastery and living in the moment that gave him a peak experience. It wasn't his first experience of flow. He had by his own admission become addicted to it as a child, and it has been like a golden thread connecting the important things in his life together.

[16.] Eddie Jordan OBE, Irish entrepreneur & investor, founder of Jordan F1 Racing Team.

6.2. Flow Motivation Indicators

FLOW MOTIVATION

INDICATORS

Seeks progress and thrives on momentum. Seeks 'The Zone'. Pursues mastery. Capability for high levels of focus. Hard working. Easily absorbed in making things better. Actively seeks skills. Visualises the ideal, though rarely achieves it. Often inclines towards perfectionism. Appreciates rare moments of harmony (with self, nature, animals). Happy with solitude, especially when pursuing mastery. Present. High appetite for risk when perfect moments are available as the reward.

FIRED UP BY

Being challenged. Excitement. Being in the zone. Freedom. Independence. Significance. Momentum. A feeling of being at one with something (for example, a surfer being part of the water or a skier feeling at one with the mountain). Perfect timing. Synchronicity. Physical challenge. Rhythm. Complete immersion. Goldilocks level of challenge.

FLAME EXTINGUISHED BY

Micromanagement. Physical constraints and lack of activity. Lack of progress or opportunity for improvement. Interruptions that break concentration. Lack of challenges. Lack of opportunity to excel at something. Zero risk. Working without a vision of the end result. Sameness. Too much certainty.

6.3 Flow – The Genius State

We can all get into flow. It's a state of being that can unleash our greatest potential. Flow allows brilliance to flow through us. It's almost as if those moments of genius are coming from somewhere else; whether that's sensing what the wind is going to do next, feeling the turn of the stock market as you watch the Bloomberg ticker on a screen or standing on stage giving a speech.

I get moments of flow when I'm on stage in front of an audience. When I'm in flow, things come out of my mouth that are unscripted, unrehearsed, and I usually have no idea where they came from. It is as if there is someone else in charge of what I'm saying; that's when the best content comes out and I add the most value. When I look back at the videos of a keynote, I often don't even remember saying the things that just flowed out. Those are moments when I was in flow and the words weren't really coming from me, they were coming **through** me.

Paul Adamson didn't start his habit of seeking flow on a super-yacht. He started at his local sailing club. He rode his bicycle down to a lake as a boy, and he recalled his first experience of flow as if it were yesterday, " I fell in love with the freedom, I could go where I wanted to go, and I loved being out in the elements. I became so addicted to sailing that I would skip school and leave a note for my Mum to say I've missed the bus again. I'd strap my sail, my rudder, and my daggerboard onto my back, get on my bike and cycle down to the sailing club and just sail all day. When you're out there on the water, all your senses come alive. You're looking at the water, so you can read the wind. You can feel the wind in your face and in your hair. You can feel the boat underneath you as you lean out with your body to counteract the wind. The wind is never constant, it's always shifting. It's just pure freedom. That's the only way I can describe it."

What Paul is describing is FLOW

FINDING FLOW IS ABOUT FINDING FREEDOM

His first moment of flow out on the water helped him escape his troubles at home and he accidentally discovered something that put him in the zone. That desire for flow has stayed with him even though he has had a major career change. Probably because of his challenges at home (his father struggled with mental illness so there were constant emotional challenges that he didn't understand when he was young), Paul developed a severe stutter as a child. It's no surprise to hear that whatever he said at home always seemed to be the wrong thing, and he got torn off a strip whenever he did things wrong. I doubt anyone expected Paul, the stutterer to speak for a living when he grew up, but in a triumph of education and determination over adversity, he's now a very successful professional speaker and flies all over the world giving keynote speeches about sales and leadership to blue-chip companies.

What struck me about Paul's story is how much of a negative effect criticism has on people. It took years for Paul to shake off his hesitancy and the consequent stutter that plagued his earlier years.

Now researchers can see our brains in action with new technology, and we start to understand more about the neuroscience, it becomes much easier to know why we react so badly to criticism. It's our fight or flight reflex that gets put on high alert. Once a person has a fear trigger set off, (and that trigger can be as simple as someone scowling at them or continually criticising to the point where they have to tread on eggshells – I'm sure you have seen that at work!), your brain starts to protect you by flooding itself with chemicals that put you on high alert of greater potential dangers to come.

In a terrific article by Benjamin Croft, founder of the World Business and Executive Coach Summit, I was staggered to read that the neuro-chemical reaction that puts you on the defensive can last between 13 and 26 hours. Just imagine what must happen when there are repeated triggers set off before the first flood of chemicals has had a chance to diminish. When you are in that state, the parts of your brain needed for clear thinking, empathy, and social interactions actually shut down. You go into survival and self-protection mode. You don't need to be the

Brain of Britain to work out that when you are flooded with cortisol and reacting like that to every little stimulus you aren't going to enjoy work, be at your best, or be fun to be around.

I'm sure you have experienced being close by someone who is in that state. It's not a nice place to be. It's an energy that's catching. When one person behaves like that it doesn't take long for everyone in close proximity to start feeling fearful too. The negativity spreads. It's a physical thing, not just an emotional one. Now we can see inside people's brains we know what's going on. It's scary stuff.

No wonder we get touchy and take time to wind down after a stressful day. Many of us are living in an almost permanent state of fear. No wonder the main reason people leave jobs isn't down to bad companies, it's because of bad managers.

Back to the sailor and speaker Paul Adamson. During his interview, Paul talked about that feeling of his best content just 'appearing from nowhere' when he's on stage, and how he gets a similar high from his work on stage as he once got from sailing.

He has been reproducing those flow moments in his life ever since, now he just finds them in different ways; speaking on stage and working with sales teams. He is still just as focused on re-creating that feeling of flow as he ever was. The subject matter might have changed but what he is looking for from his daily experience hasn't.

Your inspired moments of genius often come during your flow moments. Seek them, treasure them and capture the thoughts and ideas you have during them. They will be your best work.

6.4 Are You Flow Motivated?

Before you can answer that question, it would probably help you to know a little more about what flow motivation is and how it works.

Flow motivation is when you seek moments of flow more than you seek anything else. It's about being in the moment, about being fully present in the process more than you value the result. Some people refer to flow as 'being in the zone'.

For Flow motivated people, the very act of doing the something that puts you in the zone is more important than any outcome you get from it. When you are motivated to seek flow, what you are looking for isn't a result; it's the action itself. If you get a tangible result, then that's just a bonus, but if you don't get a result, then that's OK too.

In summary, flow motivation is when the process itself takes higher precedence than what happens because of it.

Flow happens on many levels. The experience ranges that a moment of intense focus that causes you to block the world out for a moment while you are entranced with something, (you could just be washing every last speck of coffee stain off a cup you really care about), right through to a deep meditation where you have put yourself in total control of your conscious state. There's a scale of flow. It's not a fixed thing.

We have all experienced it. Anytime when the time seems to have flown by because you have been so mentally or physically absorbed in something is a time when you have been in a flow state to some degree. When you are in maximum flow, there's a feeling of total ease, effortlessly performing at your peak and you can even feel almost superhuman. It's when the work or activity comes **through you** rather than **from you.**

For people whose prime motivation is to find flow, here's what's most important: Find the entry point into the flow zone, which is probably a process which they perfect over the years (routines really matter to flow people) and then staying in flow for as long as possible. Flow is an elusive state, but if it's your prime motivational flame, you are likely to either design your life around finding it or daydream that you could.

What doesn't matter so much is:

- Who else is involved (indeed if anyone is there at all)
- What the result or outcome of the activity turns out to be
- If the moment leads to anything or anywhere specific

All that matters is that there is an opportunity to get into the zone and enjoy every mind-bending moment of it. It's simply a state of optimally experiencing a moment in time. It's a peak performance state. Flow is about living in the moment, and that moment has to be wholly absorbing. When the moment is so riveting and enthralling, flow-driven people are happy to spend nine hundred and ninety-nine minutes of searching to experience just one minute of it.

Here's something extraordinary about flow and why it tends to lead to mastery. When you work towards finding more moments of it, you are increasing your technical competence even when things aren't flowing. That increased competence leads to a more significant proportion of your time being spent in flow over time; that's because when you practice anything for long enough, much of the effort turns from conscious skill into unconscious skill. It's when you are performing without overthinking that the performance often feels almost effortless – even if there is a great deal of actual effort involved.

If you have ever been absorbed in something to such an extent that the rest of the world and all your problems dropped away for that moment, then you know exactly what I'm talking about.

If you have flow people in your team or in your company, then they have very unique qualities. They are likely to be some of your most creative and passionate people with a powerful ability to spot patterns and connect ideas together in a way that most other people struggle to do.

They may be your most brilliant and exciting team members too, because they are always seeking things out. The flip side of this is that they can be easily distracted, have fluctuating moods and move rapidly from being highly social to being introspective and intense. Understanding more about the flow state and what drives these brilliant people can help you make the most of their potential and help them tap into their flow as often as possible.

6.5 The Science Behind Flow

The state of flow itself is not new and wasn't invented. It happens quite naturally and has been a long-recognised concept as a key element, particularly in eastern philosophies. Until it was studied in the west and backed up with science, it was just an idea, and as we didn't have the equipment to prove it was real, it was largely labelled as something fluffy and outside the mainstream. Thankfully, science has shown that flow is more than an idea; it's a measurable peak state of being that can be scientifically viewed by modern scanning technology. Psychologists define flow as "a mental state of operation in which a person performing an activity is fully immersed in a feeling of energised focus, full involvement, and enjoyment in the process of the activity"[17].

When you are in flow certain parts of your brain almost switch off, and other parts light up like a Christmas tree. The patterns are unlike anything we see in any other brain scans.

Like many important discoveries, the science of flow appeared after rather strange beginnings. After the 2nd world war, Europe was a place still reeling from the suffering, and its young population traumatised by conflict. One 16-year-old boy, traumatised by the war and not long released from an Italian prison camp found himself in a Swiss ski resort with no snow, no money, and nothing to do.

He didn't have enough cash to get a ticket to see a movie but saw in the newspaper that there was a free talk about flying saucers happening in Zurich. He was a curious young man who was already consciously looking for ways to improve his experience of life after a torrid war, but as yet hadn't found it despite various forays into religion, philosophy, and various other sources of ideas. Nothing was really helping him. The boy's name was Mihaly Csikszentmihalyi.

The talk he saw advertised flying saucers, and although he wasn't interested in the idea of finding out if there were, (as he put it) little

---

17. https://en.wikipedia.org/wiki/flow_(psychology)

green men, he was bored, poor and looking for something free to keep him amused. He went to the talk.

The talk turned out to be all about how the damage of war had affected people and how they had started to project their feelings onto some odd things because of the stress of war.

It turned out, purely by accident, that he had stumbled into a psychology lecture with the legendary pioneer, Carl Jung. He was captivated. After the lecture he read all Jung's books and the young Hungarian decided to go to the United States to study psychology. Mihaly Csikszentmihalyi is one of the founding fathers of a field now called positive psychology, and he wrote a seminal book called *Flow: The Psychology of Happiness*. It's a foundation work for social scientists, sports people, business leaders, and high performers from many fields and gives insights into how we can get into an optimal state for being our best selves.

Flow is an altered state of mind that's rooted in our biology. It's a physical change in our brain that neurobiologists can now measure. The latest research tells us that when you are in flow, there are three things that happen to your brain:

1) Your pre-frontal cortex virtually shuts down, and as a result, the things that part of your brain normally does (such as managing complex processes like reason, logic, problem-solving, planning, and memory) stops getting in the way of your performance. In other words, you stop judging yourself and are totally in the moment. The scientists call this "Transient hypofrontality".

2) Your brain is flooded with naturally produced performance-enhancing chemicals such as norepinephrine, dopamine, anandamide, serotonin and endorphins. These super-chemicals give you the ability to tap into extraordinary levels of focus, and better pattern recognition and massively amplifies your ability to tap into your natural creativity and learn new things rapidly.

3) Your brain waves change. During your routine waking existence your brain is functioning with electrical beta brain waves, but when you are in flow, your brain waves shift to slower waves that sits somewhere between alpha waves (more like a daydreaming mode) and theta waves which are what your brain does when you are in REM sleep.

The common language *I've had a brainwave* isn't just a figure of speech. It is actually quite real. When you are in flow, you have more moments of pure inspiration. A type of brain-wave called a gamma spike is something that happens during beta brainwave periods. The human experience of a gamma spike is a sudden insight or revelation.

Now you know that, you can always show your friends how much you know about neuroscience by telling them you have had a gamma spike instead of an insight. They might be rare insights, but they are less rare if you spend a good percentage of your time in flow. It explains why so many of our ah-ha moments happen when we aren't focusing on a task. Often these moments happen while we are driving, in the shower or taking time out. Archimedes had his big ah-ha moment in the bath.

Now you know why.

6.6 Isn't Everyone Flow Motivated?

There is a proportion of people on this planet who seek flow to the point where finding and experiencing it as often as possible for as long as possible ranks more highly than anything else. The feeling of being in the zone ranks higher than even family responsibilities, (think of the mountain climbers who leave wives and children at home to climb Everest ...), or extrinsic reward (for example, people who stay in jobs with low pay and poor prospects just so they still have time/space to run marathons or some other flow activity). Whether it's surfing waves in Hawaii, skiing the Eiger in Switzerland, diving in the sea to marvel at a coral reef or simply having the rest of the world fading from awareness as you look down a microscope.

It is true to say that almost everyone on the planet will, at some point, have experienced flow. It's also fair to say that everyone will have enjoyed it, but not everyone will be motivated to find more of it as their primary purpose in life. There is a good chance that people who learned early on in life to enjoy the sensations of a flow state and who got it by doing physical activity, will continue to seek that sort of action through life or something that gives them a similar buzz. The source of the thrill might change, but getting the buzz is still the important thing. One of the marked characteristics of flow is that it's deeply personal. You can't share a flow moment. It's yours and yours alone. Flow is a solitary experience. It doesn't mean that you can't be with others when you have it, it's just that you will be focused on what you are doing, not on them, when it happens.

For example, when I was a kid, I remember a feeling of losing myself when I was on skis. That total feeling of being at one with my mind, body and my environment. Naturally, I couldn't articulate it that way when I was 12 or 13, but I certainly remember moments like that over 40 years later. I enjoy skiing even now. I still get into flow doing it, and I have great fun when I ski with a group. But the group never shares my flow. Some of us get into it, and some of us don't. How we experience it is uniquely individual. Many people I know just ski because of the social aspect, some do it to conquer their fear of speed or heights, and some (like my long-suffering husband) do it because they feel they should. Not everyone gets into flow skiing.

It's no accident that I still get my downtime kicks in the same way, even though my joints complain about it a bit. Over time, I have learned other strategies for getting into flow. Writing this book for example. I get lost when I write. There is no doubt that penning something of interest to me and doing the research required to do it induces an altered state. The reason I'm sharing that is that it shows that once you have repeated experiences of flow, there are lots of ways to access it.

Professional speaker Robert Craven[18] (who you met earlier when we were talking about getting in the zone on demand), is undoubtedly in a flow state when he is on stage doing his day job. That's what makes his speaking performances seem so effortless even though I know that it takes years of thought, preparation, research, rehearsal and practice to get that good, but when you have the skills, the confidence and the preparation, flow is much more likely to happen. When Robert is out there in front of an audience, the rehearsed part of him drops away, and he gets in flow. It's mesmerising; not just for him but for everyone watching and listening to his performance. He also looks for flow experiences in his leisure time by playing guitar and painting. Both are activities that neuroscientists have proven induce the brainwave patterns of flow. There's more about artistic pursuits later when we start exploring expression motivation – but for the time being what's important for you to recognise is that people who get into flow regularly centre good chunks of their lives around getting more of it.

How might that impact the rewards you might give someone for doing a good job? For starters, it would indicate that flow motivated people are probably going to value experiences over 'things'. Just that knowledge has huge potential for how you recognise and reward people. Just asking about hobbies can give you a reliable indication if flow motivation is a strong driver.

What's also worth noting is that there are some flow substitutes that aren't quite so healthy. Flow is an altered brain state, and a similar state can be induced by the use of alcohol, tobacco, drugs, and risk-taking.

Some people love flow, but just don't associate it with the day job! My research tells me that it's more common for self-employed people and business owners to experience flow because they are more able to choose their daily work environment and have more direct control over their activities. Flow isn't generally induced inside an office cubicle when someone else is directing your every move. However, some office

---

18. www.directorscentre.com and www.robert-craven.com

jobs induce it. Software coding, solving complex intellectual or mathematical problems, and city trading also get you into a flow state. The key thing to look out for is the reduction of awareness of everything outside the task. It's exhilarating.

Flow is a by-product of a specific set of stimuli, brain chemistry, and context. There is no doubt that although it is available to us all, it is much easier to find yourself in flow when doing certain specific types of activity.

For example, it is much easier to find yourself in a flow state when you are engaged in an activity that uses your physical body and your brain at the same time. When you are just sitting using your brain, the task is going to have to be perfectly aligned with your interests to absorb you that much. That's because the coordination required for physical activity distracts parts of your brain that is often responsible for blocking your flow.

So, although it's true that the other 5 flames can also put you in a flow state from time to time, you aren't driven to seek flow at the expense of most other factors.

For example, someone who is highly flow motivated will often sacrifice many other things to get it; surfers, horse-riders and skiers know this drive well (just ask their patient spouses – if they were ever able to stay still for long enough to get married!).

6.7 The Ski-Bum Factor

An archetypal ski-bum will spend vast amounts of time on the slopes looking for those flow moments. Moments when the only objective is to experience one or more of those perfect turns when the skis glide effortlessly, and your body feels a rush of gravity and chemicals that make you feel almost weightless. Skiing through fresh snow in flow; you leave a beautiful track that won't be there for long; the wind, fresh snow or the sun will quickly fade them, but looking back up the mountain at your beautifully formed curved tracks is a profoundly satisfying feeling.

So sometimes there is a visible result (tracks), but you would ski anyway – even if you didn't leave any tracks behind. So it is with many of the activities that give us flow. Sometimes we get a result from being in flow, but **flow itself** is the result we are seeking. Anything else that happens because of those moments of flow is a bonus.

For someone who has flow as the most important driver, everything in life revolves around flow moments. For example, for a flow driven person who has chosen to ski as their method of finding flow, most primary decisions are made around the next ski-fix; where they travel, what job to do (that allows them the freedom they need), what to eat, and even where and when to sleep to maximise their skiing time and performance. A truly addicted ski-bum will sacrifice financial stability, relationships and almost everything else for those amazing moments. The only purpose of money is to fund the next ski experience. Sure, if life transpires that he or she can get paid to be closer to the snow, then that's great. In truth, most of the ski bums' decisions will be based around getting the next ski fix.

You can substitute the word SKI for just about anything that induces flow. For example, I have an uncle who is a rock guitarist who has sacrificed all sorts of things to keep doing what he loves best – even when he was being ripped off by managers, struggling financially between tours and even driving a taxi in New York City so he could eat. Despite the fact he is good enough at what he does to tour with some of the biggest names in music (The Monkees, Rainbow, Bad Company, Alice Cooper and many more) he is in the business of playing music, not of being in business. He's not interested in that side of things. He just wants to play. There is nothing that will stop him doing what he loves best. When he is in the recording studio or on stage, he is in flow, and he will sacrifice almost anything to keep doing it.

Do you have something that means so much to you that you would sacrifice most other things to keep doing it? Is it something that only you can experience? Does it have a physical element to it? Does the rest of the world and its troubles drop away when you are fully absorbed in it? If the answer is yes, you are almost certainly flow driven and will have been nodding and smiling to yourself all the way through this chapter.

If that's not you, then you have had an insight into the world of people who love things so much that they become obsessed with them. I hope it will help you to have a deeper appreciation of what they have to offer and find them a touch less frustrating in the future.

To circle back to Daniel Pink's theory for a moment, the mastery element he talked about is a big part of flow. That's because knowledge feeds itself every-time a trigger is set that leads to a little improvement. That, in turn, improves the mastery that leads to more flow. It's a virtuous circle.

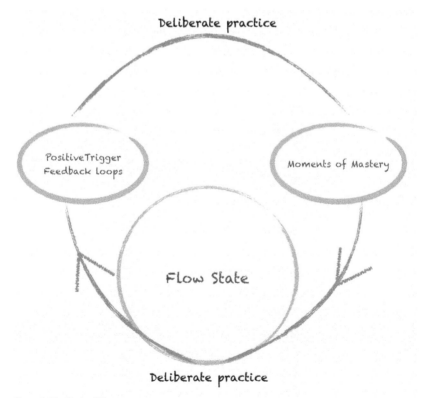

Figure 2: The Circle of Flow

Flow drive is not always an easy thing to understand from the outside. What makes it even more frustrating (and more addictive) is that flow is not very predictable. If you like a high level of certainty in your life, then it's probably not your biggest motivator. Flow would be way too elusive for that, and the irony is that the harder you try to find it, the more evasive it gets. You can't make flow happen to you; you just get on with life until it next appears.

The Unpredictable Nature of Flow

The fact that flow moments are fleeting and can't be bottled is almost the whole point. Part of the thrill and excitement is never knowing when the next moment will happen. That only serves to intensify the experience of those peak moments.

Most people aren't obsessed with finding flow. Sure, we are all grateful when we get it, and undoubtedly many of us seek it out. So even though we might enjoy flow, we don't run our careers and our social lives around it in every way. Our entire world doesn't revolve around getting our next moment of flow. So now you can see that being primarily flow motivated and simply enjoying flow when it arrives is **not** the same thing.

6.8 Flow Careers Are In Demand

Now you know that flow is genuine, you can understand why some of the most sought-after careers involve high levels of flow. Unsurprisingly, these are highly competitive areas to get into and generally require that you have at least one of the other motivational flames to be highly operational as well. More about the other flames and desirable combinations later. For now, here are some jobs that provide high levels of flow: athletes, researchers, gardeners, speakers, pilots, philosophers, monks, yoga teachers, hypnotherapists, wildlife wardens, chefs, zookeepers, computer programmers, dancers, engineers, cosmologists, florists, painter/decorators and singers.

That is quite an eclectic list, isn't it? Some of those jobs are easier to get than others, and obviously not everyone doing one of those jobs spends all their time in flow. Remember that it's almost impossible to spend all your time in flow anyway. What all those occupations have in common is a sense of deep involvement and absorption, and many of the tasks involved as key to the role have a physical element. If a high degree of time is spent in coordination with others (for example singers in a choir rather than soloists or dancers who are part of a group), there is the likelihood of high levels of inclusion motivation and of expression motivation going on as well. Remember, the brainwave states of flow are a solo activity.

It's the physical part that helps to get the brain out of the way and encourages those slow brain waves to activate and in turn, leads to the chemical flood that makes you feel great.

There is something intrinsically satisfying about elements of these jobs, and the output is clear for all to see; a medal, a clean lion enclosure or a beautiful, tidy garden. The flow ends up producing a result almost by accident. Flow people have the capability for intense focus to get results because they use that focus to achieve a level of mastery and mastery has a habit of producing a high output.

6.9 The Twins: Mastery & Flow

When we are given time to focus on something we get the opportunity to get deeply involved in what we are doing. That ability to focus is one of the critical components of becoming an expert or highly proficient at almost anything. You need to work out the best way to do something, the most productive paths to take mentally and physically, and then be able to test things out using trial and error. It's a fundamental component of learning to do anything, and it takes time. Lots of time.

Swedish psychologist K. Anders Ericsson suggested that it takes 10,000 hours of deliberate practice to develop a world-class level skill (an idea popularised by Malcolm Gladwell in his book Outliers) and as with anything academic the theory has been challenged since with a more specific notion of *deliberate practice*. That's where you stretch your skill level every time you practice. Mastering anything takes a great deal of time and focus. When you focus for significant amounts of time, there's a good chance you will start experiencing flow.

You can't force flow, but you can engineer the likelihood of it. Choose to get world-class at something. Focus and spend time working towards mastery of it – and flow will find you.

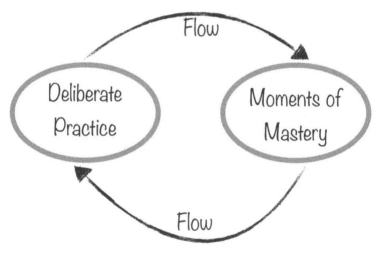

6.9 Enemies of Flow

Many of us do jobs that don't provide much opportunity for flow, or we do have jobs that could give us flow, but we rarely get the chance to get into it.

Enemy No. 1 – Distractions

The modern-day workplace is full of constant distractions, interruptions and challenges to our focus. It's like a bucket of cold water being perpetually poured over our flow flame. If you don't like having your concentration broken just when you are on the verge of getting something exactly right or connecting a series of powerful new ideas in your mind, then just think of your colleagues next time you pop over to them to break their train of thought. You might just be unintentionally breaking their flow state just when they were about to come up with a genius idea that could transform the company!

The other skill to learn is to simply say no to being distracted. Recently I was on a train to London and was sitting next to a guy called Neil, a software engineer. He had been working on a complex problem on a piece on a transport network control system for three days. He was deep into the thinking required to solve it and knew he was on the edge of a breakthrough. He described to me how the picture in his mind was starting to take shape, but he wasn't quite ready to order it and articulate it so he could send instructions to the programmers. He was still in the middle of a step-by-step mental process that always needs to be executed to get the right answer. He was in full flow. At least he was until his manager strode confidently to his desk and told him to divert to another project with a different problem.

"Earlier in my career I would have agreed and lost a ton of time, and the best solution by doing what I was told, but I instinctively knew that I was only a few hours, (at most), away from an elegant solution that would free my mind so I could give total focus to the next problem". Neil told his manager that it would slow both projects down, cause the department to underperform and that he would attend to it with his full focus when the current problem had been solved. He turned politely away and continued with his work. The manager was stunned into silence and walked away giving Neil the impression that he didn't know what to say or do next. Neil was able to get back to his work, solve the problem before the end of the day and move to the next focus.

It was an artful "no" that took courage but gave everyone on the project what they needed, and Neil was able to stay in flow (just!) and then take a break and move on to the next project knowing he had solved a big problem. He finished his day satisfied and happy. That was one fun train journey.

Just increasing your awareness of flow can make you a better person to work with, work for and learn from.

There's something to consider about the supposedly 'depressing' image of a 'boring' office. Just because people are sitting in booths and not talking to each other, (often pictured as the epitome of depressing work environments on TV and in films), doesn't mean they aren't enjoying what they are doing – but if people focus on their work for too long without a break, flow can turn into burnout. The phrase "burnout" was coined by American psychologist Herbert Freudenberger in the 1970's when he was investigating levels of sickness and stress in medical professionals, and it's something we all need to be aware of, so we can do our bit to avoid personal burnout and to be conscious of signs of it in others.

Enemy No. 2 – Lack of Activity

Two of the key attributes of a flow state include an intense and focused concentration on the present moment (which explains why we drink so much coffee at work . . .) and the merging of action and awareness. It's the second one that's important to consider for this enemy of flow. Some people think that it's not possible to combine office work and activity, but some research by my friend and PhD candidate Elizabeth Nelson suggests otherwise. Elizabeth goes into detail in her recent book *The Healthy Office Revolution.*[19] She was able to quantify the effect of exercise in the office, just by providing a step tracker and stationary bikes and employees showed a 12%[20] improvement in task performance. There were also some surprising side effects of wearing exercise trackers to measure steps taken. Her data showed that people started to relate to each other face-to-face more because they would get up and walk to someone's desk rather than send an email. That may have broken flow from time to time, but it did result in stronger relationships between workers in the office.

[19.] http://www.thehealthyofficerevolution.com
[20.] Activity versus no activity 5-10 minutes on a stationary bike seat until they felt their heart rate was elevated, but not hot or sweating.

Enemy No. 3 – Poor Diet and Snacking Habits

Remember that flow is a combined physical and mental state, so your brain needs the right fuel to get into it. Once again, Elizabeth Nelson's research data gives us valuable insights. By switching research participants from eating cream filled doughnuts to consuming an avocado and spinach smoothie (now, there's dedication for you …) there was a 45% improvement in task performance when people were tested 25 minutes after snacking. Evidently, there is a connection between what we eat and how we perform. I believe we are only just starting to take action about this in our workplaces, but we still have a long way to go. Many of us are still fuelled by sugar and caffeine; guilty as charged.

The research also indicates that introducing natural elements to our offices increases task performance by 10% – and even artificial plants and pictures of the outdoors gave the same results as real plants. It's no coincidence that many flow activities happen outdoors, but we can improve our interior environments as well.

Enemy No. 4 – Lack of Challenge or Progress Towards Mastery

Work doesn't have to be full of meaning, but it does have to have an element of challenge for us to get into flow. An example of this is that video gamers get into flow; in fact, it's a problem for many. Flow can tip over into addiction. There is a point when people tip over from flow into something psychologists call hyper-focus. That's when we get so pleasurably absorbed by one aspect of something that we lose focus on the big picture.

Remember that the key point about flow motivation is the process itself rather than the result. Flow people can get almost *over* absorbed in the task itself and lose focus on the *outcome*. Everything has a yin and yang. Mastery is great, but in a work environment, the end result needs to be kept in mind.

6.10 Meaningful Flow

Your flow moments are likely to be some of the peak memories of your life so far. What is interesting is this. Even though flow is a fleeting and ephemeral moment in time that can't be captured or bottled, flow moments are often such powerful experiences, we tend to reflect on them and recall them as significant moments. People then have a tendency to do something very interesting with those memories; we add meaning to them, and those memories become very precious to us. They become a part of who we are and the journey we have taken.

In a working environment that has significant implications. Flow people can produce the most amazing work, especially when they created it during flow. Those outputs can be close to genius. In fact, I have a firm belief that moments of brilliance are flow moments – captured.

As managers and leaders, we need to recognise the massive importance that people attach to the things that they produced when they were in flow.

As Dan Ariely says inside his book *Payoff*, acknowledgement is a kind of 'human magic'. Moments of flow may be personal, but the impact will ripple out to the company and other team members. If managers don't acknowledge the effort and give no meaning to their activities, then the flow either stops or those moments of genius will walk out of the door to somewhere where their flow moments are more greatly appreciated.

Flow is a sort of genius. It's often when we learn our greatest positive life lessons or produce our best work. So, despite the fact we can't capture flow itself, we do capture the lessons and the meaning of it. Now that's something worth cherishing.

6.11 Flow Summary

So, what have we learned about Flow?

- Flow is a natural human state of peak performance that can be reproduced given a set of known triggers.
- Flow produces emotional and physical highs that are hard to beat.
- Personal flow is dependent on creating the time and space to concentrate with a clear outcome in mind, the ability to focus with intensity and having a Goldilocks level of challenge.
- Group flow is dependent on trust, ease of communication, mutual respect, similar skill levels, and a Goldilocks level of project or challenge with a level of risk and reward that make it worth focusing on
- Signs of it are: Unspoken competence and high engagement. Think of a steamy gym full of pro athletes who know exactly what they need to get done. It's a positive addiction to feedback, progress and success.
- Upsides are: Great quality work. Engaged people with pride for their projects. Highly creative environment. High level of work satisfaction.
- Downsides are: Individual flow is solitary. Need to balance with team flow.

6.12 Flow Black Belt Strategies

Remember Mr Csikszentmihalyi? The research by the modern father of flow tells us exactly how to create the ideal environment and conditions for flow. We can use these at work and in our private lives to enhance our experience.

The seven conditions that Csikszentmihalyi tells us that promote flow are:

- Identifiable goals and clearly identifiable rules
- The time and space to concentrate on a narrow focus of attention
- The ability to respond instantly to feedback from your activity
- A balance between ability and challenge (the Goldilocks zone of an activity being neither too taxing nor too easy)
- No worry about failure
- The ability to step beyond self-consciousness for periods
- A high degree of personal autonomy and control over the activity

When these things come together, we experience a sense of unstoppable momentum. A sense of perpetual progress kicks in, and we refuel our energy levels from the inside out. That's the other thing about flow. It reignites you mentally and physically. That's really helpful because we don't stay in flow all the time. That would be almost impossible. When the inevitable dips happen, you are then in a place where you can accept them as part of the progression of getting from where you are to where you want to be.

To generate more flow, the big word to remember is to give yourself the conditions to FOCUS. If you are managing or leading others, then it's up to you to create the conditions where flow has the best possibility of happening. Minimise distractions, interruptions and where possible, give people the chance to find physical space that allows them to be more creative. You need blood to the brain to get into flow and sitting in one place staring at one screen with your eyes being strained by pixels is not the best way to get peak performance. But you know that already . . .

Practical Checklist for Flow

- Keep distractions to a minimum. Focus is everything.
- Get really good at something, however unconnected it appears to be with work. For example, being an ace squash player, knitter, skier or craft baker in their time off will bring multiple new skills to the job and a mindset of accepting challenges.
- Listen to people. Allow them to think on the outside of their heads and be ready capture the creative solutions that come out.
- Avoid editing or critique other people's thinking before it's fully formed. Allow people to think using randomly connecting ideas and solutions.
- Keep your environment free from too much clutter or mess.
- Introduce plants to the workspace! Nature induces flow
- Encourage and provide healthy snacks and nutrition (can be as simple as supplying water jugs with attractive looking fruit or herbs floating in it next to the coffee machines to offer a brain-healthy alternative)
- Allow people to choose their own challenges and keep it within the Goldilocks zone

Flow at Work

Here are some suggestions to encourage flow in a company setting:

- Zone your workspaces where possible so people can find quiet space if they need it to get into the flow zone
- Help people understand the concept of flow, and its relationship with doing great work that is intrinsically satisfying
- Avoid mixing too many skill levels inside one project. Some people will get bored while others will be overstretched. If the gaps between the skills are too wide, the group won't flow; it will fracture
- Encourage good working habits such as encouraging time stretching, moving, and time away from the desk in a structured way, flow needs blood-flow!

- Progressive communication, always listening always moving forward, no one excluded from the conversation. Conversational and communication momentum is a requirement for team flow
- Group flow only happens between people when there is an unspoken language of understanding and anticipation of the moves of others so encourage clear role allocations with flexible boundaries during high stakes projects.
- Provide stories and metaphors for the team to buy into to create a standard team language, it shortens the communication requirements.

6.14 Why Flow Alone Isn't Enough

Csikszentmihalyi described flow as 'the science of optimal experience'. So, if we are fired up to achieve flow (or have even have a small taste of it), why aren't we **all** fired up all the time by working to get more of it?

There must be other forces at work. First of all, there's a cost to finding flow. We all have competing, and often conflicting priorities that means finding flow has to drop down the list of what we spend our days doing. Pesky things sometimes get in the way; things like earning a living and the daily distractions of life that are inevitable for most of us.

We have other needs too. We need to connect with people, and flow is a relatively solitary activity. As wonderful as flow is, it does not give us everything we need to be happy and successful. We can't achieve those things in a vacuum. We are social creatures. We have evolved to work as teams and to co-operate with each other. Further than that, we have developed to love and have empathy for each other. So as much fun and as addictive as flow might be, it's not the only game in town.

So, the next pillar of drive is all centred on our fundamental need to connect with other people. It's our deep-seated need to be included in a family, team, community, or peer group. That leads us neatly onto the next Motivational Flame ...

Chapter 7

Inclusion Motivation

7.1 The Inclusion Flame

Doctors are a rare commodity outside the cities in Nicaragua. Rural areas there don't have much in the way of medical help, and even if they did, many people who live in the countryside couldn't afford treatment and medicines anyway. Almost half of the rural population live in extreme poverty.[21] So when a pair of European doctors arrived in a remote village it was inevitable they were going to find people who needed their help.

Dr Nick Snelling was one of those doctors. Back home in the UK, Dr Snelling is a GP (General Practitioner). He tends his local patients under the UK's National Health Service system in Bristol, a vibrant hub city in the West of England. For Nick, Central America on horseback is not exactly home from home, he's a volunteer medic who takes time out of his home life to help disadvantaged communities.

The remote village he was visiting on this trip was miles away from the nearest small town. The local transport link consisted of a series of boats or a very long walk to the nearest town. Just imagine for a moment what it must be like to live in a place where you have to trek miles through the jungle just to reach a small town with a doctor, and then know that even if you made it – you can't afford to be treated. If you or your kids get sick, then there's not much left to do other than hope and pray.

That's exactly what Dr Snelling met with when he got to the village that day, "We rode in on our horses. The place was pretty inaccessible. One of the first patients we saw was a baby boy. His parents brought

---

[21.] According to the World Health Organisation.

him in. He was a tiny little thing and very ill. When I started to ask about him, we soon discovered that the child was one of twins and the other baby was sick too, so we sent dad back to get the other child. Both children turned out to be critically ill."

The doctors worked quickly and did everything they could with the facilities they had. Despite their best efforts, they had arrived too late to save the first little boy, but the other baby survived.

"Had we not ridden in that day I'm certain that poor family would have lost both of their children."

Making A Difference to Others

That's inclusion motivation right there, and Nick is driven by it. He spends months of his private time helping other people without pay. He has a passion for bringing care to remote communities, so they can stay in their own villages, "It's a real privilege to be a doctor, to go into these communities and help these people, to be valued. I get to do things that are often taken for granted here in England, yet in some of the places I visit I get to see the impact – one person at a time" he said.

So where did his drive come from?

"I had a Latin teacher in school," he told me. "One day she said something that really resonated with me, she said *Do something useful every day and you will have a great life.* That hit me really hard. It changed me." He said, "I really started to think about what I was going to do with my life. It took me a long time to decide to become a doctor,[22] and even that was something that was never part of a grand plan. But I always worked on being useful."

The inclusion of people less fortunate than ourselves drives many of the social movements in our world, it guides philanthropic choices and fuels random and deliberate acts of kindness. Bringing people together and helping others is what gives us a sense of connection and is often what gives meaning to our lives.

[22.] Dr. Snelling didn't start medical school until he was in his thirties. It wasn't part of his original life plan.

7.2 Inclusion Motivation Summary Table

INCLUSION MOTIVATION

INDICATORS

Seeks company. Builds networks easily. Team player. Asks 'who' before they ask 'what', 'when' or 'how'. Demonstrates caring. Loyal. Uses inclusive language: 'we' and 'us' before they use 'me' and 'I'. Communicative. Empathetic. Outgoing. Good listener. Can be easily distracted by new people. Fun. Emotionally intelligent. Great connector. Mediator. Remembers details about people. High level of contribution to groups and communities. Optimistic views of the intentions of others. Seeks consensus.

FIRED UP BY

Personal connection. Teamwork. Collaboration. Organising groups to achieve collective success. Negotiating successful solutions. Generating rapport. Socialising. Building networks. Fairness. Mutual respect. Social harmony. Listening to others. Creating connections. Helping others fulfil their potential. Resolving conflict.

FLAME EXTINGUISHED BY

Being excluded, or powerless to change the exclusion of others. Lack of emotional connection. Selfish behaviour of others. Working solo. Loneliness. Use of power when cooperation is possible. Social injustice. Political power plays. Lack of reciprocation. Unfairness.

Keywords – Kindness, Company, People.

7.3. What Is Inclusion Motivation?

The Inclusion flame is all about people. We are social creatures; it's hardwired into us to be part of a group. That group might be a family, team, company, or village. In our workplaces, it's the cultural glue and the invisible bonds that hold groups of people, organisations and companies together. Without it, groups don't work properly.

Yet there are plenty of situations, especially in the workplace, where people either don't fit in or don't have the skills to work with others effectively. There are hundreds of reasons why people get excluded, but the central theme is that they are different and that means they don't fit into the norm. The differences that prevent inclusion might be background, education, race, gender or even something simple like dressing in a different way to the rest of the group or understanding the workplace jargon. Our workplaces are full of the unintended consequences of a lack of inclusion, and it's a source of immeasurable little miseries. So let's do something about it.

In his recent work on health, futurologist and speaker Christian Kromme noted in his recent book[23] that even individual cells react predictably when they are under threat. "When single cells are in stress, the cell membrane closes and they go into rescue mode, the cell wall thickens and the cells reduce communication with other cells. That has the effect of allowing the cell to receive less information from their environment. That reduces their ability to adapt and react, and human beings behave in exactly the same way. When we are under threat we shut down. We are less open in our communication, and we also are less able to receive information. We shut down, just like our cells shut down. Conversely, when a cell is relaxed, it's cell membrane starts to thin, and the cell absorbs information from its environment, single cells start to multiply and to socialise."

I believe that understanding reveals a great deal about how pervasive company culture is, and culture is rooted in how we relate to each other.

[23.] *Humanification - Go Digital, Stay Human.* Published by Choir Press 2017

The biology of cells and how they react have remarkable parallels too, as Christian Kromme explains. "Just like people, cells adjust to their environment. Did you know that if you place a healthy cell into a stressful and unhealthy environment, the cell will become ill, and when you put a sick cell in a healthy and stress-free environment the cell starts to recover." I know Christian's work well as we worked on his book together and I was astonished by some of the parallels between biology, technology and company culture. There is still so much we don't know, but if we look to nature for inspiration, we start to get clues. As Christian points out, "when you think about communities of people, they react in just the same way. For example, if you have two colleagues in a company department who don't communicate, trouble soon starts to appear. If the communication issue isn't solved quickly, the problem can infect the whole department, the same way as an illness can eventually affect the whole body."

So being part of a team isn't just natural at a human level, it even matters on a cellular level. Now there's something that I bet you didn't get up this morning thinking about and yet it makes perfect sense. Our own bodies are amazing machines of moving parts, messages and complex interactions with our environment and we unconsciously adapt to what's going on around us one millisecond at a time. We are not machines, we are living and adaptive organisms.

We have a deep human need to be part of a team, and that need drives many of the minute-by-minute choices we make in our lives. Being included is essential to all of us in some way, but for some people their inclusion is paramount. It's THE most important thing.

Oddly enough, they don't always *see* it that way but what they DO tells the story loud and clear.

Entrepreneur Sammy Blindell remembers being excluded, and it is one of her earliest strong memories, "On my very first day at school, I was bouncing around with excitement. I was really excited about going to school. I remember going out for the afternoon break, the sun was shining, and I could hear the noise in the playground of loads of kids having a good time. There were girls playing games and various gaggles of kids gathered around. I was only five. I remember vividly spotting a group of girls who were playing a skipping game that looked really fun, so I ran over to join in. What happened next was such a shock. One of the girls put her hand up to my face and said, "go and play somewhere else, Fatso". At that moment I was branded the fat kid. I was branded as the last person to be picked for teams. That was a real shock for me. Up until then, I was always outside playing with other kids, always involved and included. I was popular. Now I was frozen out. What I didn't realise then was it would fire me up for the rest of my career to make sure that no-one was ever labelled in the wrong way again."

Sammy now has an international business called How to Build a Brand.[24] She talks openly about how she almost cries when she hears about small businesses that get branded in the wrong way, for the wrong thing and don't get the customers they deserve; talk about having a golden thread that runs through everything you do! She has built a global community, the Brand Builders Club that connects like-minded entrepreneurs together to share their struggles and celebrate successes. Sammy's people get their message out and attract their ideal customers. You can see just what a powerful motivator Inclusion can be.

The Inclusion flame isn't just about being liked either. There are other ways we can feel included, such as by being recognised or respected. For example, a leading scientist might be happy with her papers and experiments in her laboratory working alone, but she will certainly want her work to be accepted and recognised by her peers when she makes a breakthrough. That's a scientists' way of being included. Inclusion is also nothing to do with introversion or extroversion either; it's just expressed differently depending on your personality. Some people just like being with people and love to be part of a group, while others are happy to go their own way and come together with others only when it suits them. If people are less than

---

24. www.howtobuildabrand.org

secure in their own identity or lack self-confidence (and this strikes us all at some point no matter how brave a face we might put on it!), being part of a group can be a way to feel supported by others. It also can help us educate ourselves about how to fit in more comfortably, although educating ourselves is always something that carries an element of risk. If we don't get the group accepted behaviour right, we run the risk of rejection; not everyone gets it right.

I believe that there are plenty of leaders out there who are highly skilled and have risen up the ranks because of their abilities, but are nervous in a group social situation when their expertise is no longer what they are being measured by or judged upon. That's because as people rise up the ranks, people start to assume you know the technicalities of what you do. They begin to expect different things from you like gravitas,[25] a natural air of self-confidence and the ability to make other people feel comfortable around you.

Learning to include others or develop the social intelligence to fit in with the shifting sands of complex social dynamics isn't always an easy thing to do. If you are primarily flow motivated, then you are likely to have built up your mastery by being internally focused much of the time. To suddenly be judged on other things isn't always a smooth transition to make. It comes as a shock to some people. I remember when my neighbour Charlotte Dujardin went from being an unknown rider to Olympic dressage champion overnight, she was so unprepared for the press attention and the sudden requirement to be a spokesperson for the sport, that her trainer Carl Hester had to step in and do most of the interviews on her behalf. That might be an extreme event, but it's a good analogy for the transition that people have to make when they move from being an expert to being a leader.

As leaders and managers, it's up to us to recognise those who are struggling and do our best to include them without them having to

---

25. If you want to develop your gravitas, I highly recommend Antoinette Dale Henderson's book *Leading with Gravitas* published 2015 by Rethink Press Limited.

always find their own way into the group and managing that new dynamic.

People high on the inclusion scale burn brightest when they are connecting with people or making connections. Other people are so important to them that without them, their flame goes out. They need plenty of interaction with other people or their whole world darkens.

Most people would expect Paul Brook to be an introvert and not inclusion driven (read geek) because of his job title, Director Data Analytics EMEA at Dell EMC, yet job titles can be deceptive, so I challenge you to dig a little deeper and make fewer assumptions about people and their jobs.

Paul has a high inclusion drive, and this came out during our interview very quickly. He told me that if he won the lottery and didn't go to work again, the thing he would miss the most was the fascinating people he meets because of his job, "I would deeply miss having a conversation with the head of research infrastructure at GSK, and talking with Dr Paul Collegiate, the head of HPC (High-Performance Computing) at Cambridge University. I would deeply miss being in the room when that conversation happened. I would profoundly miss meeting a lead blogger on Artificial Intelligence, having a chat with a guy who five years ago was with the US military and is now starting his own company. I would really miss meeting a guy from MasterCard and then talking to a former federal agent who was the lead investigator in the largest credit card bust of all time in the United States. I would never meet those guys if it wasn't for what I do now."

That's inclusion all the way.

The opposite of inclusion is exclusion and isolation. If you keep people in the dark, their fire goes out. Even prison isn't the worst punishment for criminality; solitary confinement takes that punishment even further. Yet, every day there are people out there in a type of invisible solitary confinement at work.

It shouldn't be that way, and we all have a responsibility to do something about it. You don't need to be a superhero and have a personality transplant to make a difference either. Part of the art of inclusion is realising that the smallest gesture from you can brighten up the day for someone else. The wonder of brightening someone else's day is you get back 1000 times more than you give. First of all, you have to light yourself up to do it (which might be a bit of an effort), you light them up by doing it and in return for being nice, you get to feel good about yourself for having done it.

As you can see, that's a triple win.

Do you need to make a grand gesture and start changing your personality and becoming something you are not? No, of course not. Just smiling at someone is a great start. In fact, if you don't normally do too much of that, then you might be pleasantly shocked at the effect it has on people. Sure, it may feel a little strange at first, but when you get used to it, you'll probably find that it feels rather good.

Just a simple smile is enough to change our biochemistry. Just walking into work and smiling at someone can change your day and theirs. We get a little shot of feel-good hormones when someone connects with us. Mark Bowden, an evolutionary and behavioural psychologist did a great TED talk[26] about smiling. In a highly amusing and revealing talk Bowden explains why only genuine smiles are effective. It's not enough to smile on the outside and be thinking something negative on the inside because the human brain picks up the minute differences in our face, eyes and body. For everyone involved, the smile needs to be genuine and to do that you have to think kind thoughts. It's not possible to be thinking horrible thoughts and smiling in a natural way at the same time. Our sub-conscious ability to read micro-expressions (those fleeting glimpses of our true intentions broadcast on our faces for milli-seconds) means that we are not as quickly taken in as some people would hope. In other words, we can spot a genuine smile at 50 paces.

If you want to look at it from a business perspective, smiling gives

---

[26] https://www.youtube.com/watch?v=rk_SMBIW1mg

you a great ROI. That's the great thing about understanding and maximising your inclusion flame; it doesn't just reward the person who gets – it rewards the giver as well. If you are already inclusion motivated, you probably already know about that.

If you are an extrovert, you will have a ton of friends. Extrovert people are great at bringing people together and enjoy the buzz and vibrancy of lots of people and the energy it brings. They are often the hosts at your local business networking group, they are the ones in the office that organise the drinks after work or the birthday celebrations, or start the collections for colleagues who are having a baby, a big birthday or who are moving on.

If you are an introvert, you may have fewer relationships, but that doesn't mean relationships don't matter! Quality over quantity is likely to be what you value most, and integrity matters a great deal. In fact, many different research papers talk about being quiet yet having high integrity as dominant leadership traits. Introverts often ensure they have the personal space and time to consider how to add value to those relationships and to only speak up when they have something brilliant to add to the equation. A more introvert Inclusion driven person still has the need for connection, but may be happier building an online community or connecting with people by writing, blogging, or finding a way of being with people in a quieter and more peaceful environment. I remember the knowing laughter of the audience when Dr Susan Cain talked about her happiest memories of family time being mostly spent sitting quietly in a room reading a treasured book[27], with other members of the family happily doing the same.

Let's be clear about introversion; it's NOT the same as shyness. It's just that introverts don't need the spotlight on themselves to feel like they are part of something. In fact, they can be brilliant at bringing people together because the focus doesn't have to be on them. Introverts are happy to shine the spotlight somewhere else. They don't

---

[27.] If you haven't seen Susan's TED talk on the quiet power of introverts, then Google it. It's a great talk and important message.

need the attention, they know who they are and what they stand for because they have processed that internally.

One very fired up introvert I know, business coach Adrian Malpass, started a hashtag that local businesses in our rural part of the UK could use to encourage locals to support their local companies and traders. It was an inspired move. The #GlosBiz® hashtag now reaches over 1.3 million people a week. Now that's serious inclusion! In his professional life, Adrian strikes an interesting balance between the importance of Inclusion drive and Results drive. When I asked him the simple question "what drives you" his answer was immediate. "Do the right thing. Integrity is everything" he said.

Values such as integrity demonstrate a high level of inclusion. That's because Inclusion drive is all about being accepted by (and doing the right thing for) others. The only way you can do that over the long term is by building a positive reputation and building trust. Adrian's long-term approach of building a community, giving before he asked for anything and contributing to his community is driven by that determination to 'do the right thing' and to connect people to each other. It's no accident that his GlosBiz® Business Breakfasts are one of the most successful business networking events for miles around. The people who attend come from the smallest local micro-businesses right through to CEO's of the region's most influential institutions, a combination that doesn't typically work in the same room.

It's this desire to include others, to connect people and to contribute that are the hallmarks of Inclusion motivation. The fact that Adrian is an introvert (and has the data to prove it!) demonstrates nicely that you don't need to be an extrovert to have the inclusion flame as your biggest motivating factor.

Whether you are introvert or extrovert what's not in doubt is that all of us are motivated by connecting with other people at some level. Marketers know just how compelling our need to connect with other people is. If you have ever seen a special offer telling you something is 'best selling', or 'ranked number one' or is 'one of last few places', then you are being influenced by inclusion (or equally if not more powerful still) the threat of exclusion. Psychologist Dr Robert Cialdini[28] terms this phenomenon Social Proof (or in his more recent works, the power of consensus.)

When you see the principle of social proof in action as part of an advertising or marketing strategy, the seller is effectively telling you that a high-status tribe is doing/buying/loving this, and if you miss out then you could end up being an outcast. So, we are all influenced by Inclusion in some way, yet for some people, it's a **primary** motivator.

Some people build teams and communities because that's what they love to do best and bringing people together is the main thing that drives them. In the business world, entrepreneurs with a high level of inclusion motivation often find themselves with loyal teams and equally loyal customers.[29]

7.4 The Woman With The Golden Touch

Judy Naake was always focused and at her best working face to face with customers; she just had an instinct for it. Brought up in a family business, she started off standing behind the shop counter of her father's business at only 4 years old, and she told me she couldn't wait to be old enough to take the money and put it in the till. She loved dealing with people.

When we first met at a business awards dinner, she politely asked me where I lived. I hesitated because usually people stare at me blankly when I respond (I live in the middle of nowhere near a series of towns few people have ever heard of), but Judy surprised me. She immediately recounted a businesswoman who had a beauty salon near my house

---

[28.] Author of *Influence: The Psychology of Persuasion* published by Harper Business.

[29.] That doesn't mean that all great leaders and are good at connecting personally. For example, the late Steve Jobs showed a great understanding of what people needed, wanted and would buy - but wasn't known (and didn't really care about) for his social skills when he was building Apple.

who she had last connected with 15 years earlier. She promptly rattled off her name; the names of her children and some of the personal woes that she remembered had been troubling her at the time. She went on to tell me that one of the secrets of her success was rooted in the fact she knew every single salon owner that she dealt with all over the country to that level. It was one of the secrets of her success.

The business had started to grow and an increasing number of beauticians shops were applying her signature product (a self-tanning formula called St. Tropez) to their clients' skin, when one day, she had a call from a disgruntled customer. Despite the 250-mile round trip ahead of her she immediately got in the car to sort the problem out. She had no idea who the customer was, but the lady was really upset because she had a streaky tan, "You have to have total faith in your product or service. If you have the choice between sorting out a problem with an existing customer or taking a new order – you sort the problem out first because that problem isn't going to go away, it's going to multiply."

When Judy arrived on the outskirts of London to help her distressed customer, she discovered that the lady was an Oscar-nominated make-up artist who had worked on the famous film Four Weddings and a Funeral. She had an important engagement coming up and so was understandably mortified by what had happened to her. That last thing that a high profile professional make-up artist needs to promote her career and capability is to be seen with a streaky tan in public. Needless to say, she appreciated the attention and the focus given by Judy to getting her problem sorted out. She and Judy are still in business together today. "Being in business is about doing the right thing", Judy told me after she recounted that story to me. There's a success theme coming out here, isn't there?

In the early days, long before Judy sold her business for around £70 million, her early business relationships were built on a foundation of friendship and trust. "I couldn't afford to buy ready-made sandwiches. My old boss at my previous company would have made the trainees I was working with (people who were being shown how to use the product properly, so they would stock it in their shops) buy their own lunch. I didn't think that was right. I advertised the training courses and when I had enough bookings, I'd book a venue and make the sandwiches myself and take them with me. I didn't want people walking out halfway through the day! I wanted to get to know them, have the chance to look them in the eye. That's how you build relationships. If people know you, like you and really trust you, they will buy anything from you. If you do that, then you can't let them down can you?"

During those sandwich lunches order forms would get passed around, Judy would answer questions and get to know the ladies, and that's how she built her business. One sandwich, one person and one order at a time; Inclusion style.

I was delighted to find out that just as this book was about to go to print that Judy had been awarded an MBE in the Queens Honours list. It couldn't have been given to a nicer person.

So inclusion is a clear-cut driver. What is less clear-cut is the degree that this inclusion flame drives our individual choices and behaviours. That's because none of the 5 flames of motivation work or play out in isolation. They are all burning in a slightly different combination and in different proportions in each of us. Our heat map is unique and deeply personal. How much you are driven by the inclusion flame is a matter of degree.

Our inclusion flame goes right back in time to the evolutionary advantages that humans get from being part of a tribe.

7.5 When Flow and Inclusion Work In Harmony

Remember speaker/skipper Paul Adamson the round-the-world yacht captain? You probably recall that he discovered his flow state when he was alone on the water as a young boy. What is interesting is that as he matured and developed as a person, he wanted other people to be able to tap into the same joy that he found when he was in flow himself. At that point, Paul became motivated by something more. He wanted to be able to transfer that wonderful experience to others, and his inclusion drive increased as he grew in his own self-confidence.

His life had moved beyond just being out on a boat on the water himself. It stretched to working as part of a team and progressed to him caring about other people's flow. With practice, he increased his skills and confidence in communicating with people and realised that he didn't need to be on the water to have a major impact. Now he is taking his message to an ever-growing audience as a highly regarded professional speaker. Not bad for someone who stuttered so badly he couldn't get his own name out a few years earlier.

Paul's inclusion flame has become progressively more important to him as he has matured. Recently, Paul was offered the opportunity to take on a major role at the famous yacht company Oyster. He accepted and is now Chief Turnaround Officer (what a great title for a yachtsman turned businessman to have!) and he is busy running the day-to-day operations of a multi-million pound company with interests all over the world that employs hundreds of people. It's wonderful to hear about great success stories like that when you know about some of the challenges that shaped the person behind the title. I'm certain that Paul will help the tide rise once again on Oyster's fortunes and help to train and employ some more master craftsmen and women once more.

Author John C. Maxwell in his book, 'The 21 Irrefutable Laws of Leadership', talks about law No. 10 – The Law of Connection. Maxwell reminds us "Leaders Touch a Heart Before They Ask for a Hand". It will be the same for you, as you develop as a person and become progressively more self-aware, you will be motivated by new things and as a result, enjoy a fuller experience of life.

Being part of a team is rooted deeply in our evolution, and where does the feeling of team start? Take a guess . . .

7.6 Tribal Ties

Being part of a team starts with being part of a family. We all start off dependent on other people. As children, we take a long time before we are strong enough and smart enough to feed ourselves and that has led humans to have a unique way of working together in groups. We have grown to rely on other people in our family and in wider tribes. It's our evolutionary survival mechanism; we have evolved to be social creatures. We are hardwired to survive and thrive in groups. From an evolutionary perspective, we have always had to rely on other people bringing food for some members of the community. Humans were hunter-gatherers long before we were farmers. We have been sitting around fires sharing food and stories for many thousands of years.

Although the Internet has changed our ability to connect socially with each other from great distances (Oh, the wonders of Skype and FaceTime), we still have an evolutionary need to share physical proximity, to share food together and share experiences with groups of other people. A sense of belonging and our need for connection to others is a fundamental part of what it means to be human.

Inclusion motivation is a part of who we all are. So, aren't we all inclusion motivated? Well, not to the same degree, and that's where things get interesting. Extremely high levels of inclusion motivation have the potential to sabotage performance in an environment where winning means others must lose; sports and some elements of business. It's a great balancing motivation though and prevents unethical behaviours creeping in.

Abraham Maslow created his hierarchy of human needs almost 100 years ago; a model that psychologists still use today. It was simplified and nicely adapted for a modern audience by the personal development guru Anthony Robbins, who described one of our core needs of his spin-off idea of "six human needs" as Love and Connection (an idea based loosely based on Maslow's work). The love and connection need is Inclusion motivation.

Richard Barrett, founder of the Barrett Values Centre and respected author on personal and corporate values also uses Maslow's original work at the starting point for his research. Why I am sharing this? To show that inclusion drive is not new, it's the engine of many of our motivations, it's just I have observed that for some people it is not just something that is important; it is THE most important thing.

I've also noticed that it's when it's lower down on the order of importance (especially when it's the 4th or 5th flame), there's a risk that priorities can shift so far in favour of results that values and behaviours start to become compromised. Insider trading, fiddling figures and poor ethical practices all stem from a low level of inclusion motivation (or a twisted version of it.)

We all need to be part of a group, or be respected and recognised by others to be fulfilled, happy, and achieve our full potential.

Inclusion is About Acknowledgement

In experiments performed by Dan Ariely, Professor of Behavioural Economics at Duke University, to assess how motivated we are by the recognition of others, Ariely and his team were able to measure the power of acknowledgement. In a carefully thought out experiment, a group of people were paid to pair up letters printed on pieces of paper and each time they did the exercise they were given a diminishing amount of money for completing the task. The first group wrote their names on their pieces of paper and were acknowledged by the collector. The second group had no names on the paper and were ignored by the collector and the third group had no names, were ignored by the collector and had their work shredded. What surprised the scientists was the power of the acknowledgement. When people were recognised and acknowledged for what they had done, even if the work was apparently meaningless, they went on working for far longer even with diminishing returns for their work. People who had their work shredded stopped working only marginally earlier than the people who weren't acknowledged. As Ariely puts it so elegantly in his book *Payoff* "... if you really want to demotivate people, shredding their work is the way to go, but that you can get almost all the way there simply by ignoring their efforts." He concludes "Acknowledgement is a kind of human magic – a small human connection, a gift from one person to another that translates into a much larger, more meaningful outcome."

The lesson that gives us is a treasure. Just acknowledging the work of others increases motivation. The 'boss' in Ariely's experiments didn't comment on the quality of the work. Indeed, he didn't even look to see if the subjects had got the letter pairing right or wrong. He was not commenting on a job well done. All he did was to acknowledge the person's existence and ask them if they wanted to repeat the job for less pay.

The experiment was carefully designed to test only for what it takes to demotivate people. So, our tribal roots run deep. We all need to be part of something and have others in our group recognise us. None of us lives in a vacuum. As a friend of mine, business coach Richard Gray says, people want "hugs and cash – in that order" – in these days of appropriate contact, of course he's talking in metaphors, but the idea is simple and spot on.

We are at our best when we are part of a constellation where everyone has a place to shine.

Coach and astrophysicist Jazz Rasool talks about the idea of stars shining brightly and having more impact when they find their place amongst others. "Few people remember the name of an individual star, but they do remember the name of the constellation." From the context, it's then possible to find the key stars inside it. It's helpful metaphor for something that the social scientists – such as Professor of Psychology and Gowen Professor in the Social Sciences at the University of Rochester, Edward L. Deci and his colleague Professor Richard Ryan describe in their 'mini-theory' about how we inter-relate, (their Relationships Motivation Theory, part of the wider Self Determination

Theory or SDT[30]). Deci and Ryan have done extensive work on their SDT framework that studies motivation and personality. SDT is a broad framework for the study of human motivation and personality, described as; "SDT articulates a meta-theory for framing motivational studies, a formal theory that defines intrinsic and varied extrinsic sources of motivation, and a description of the respective roles of intrinsic and types of extrinsic motivation in cognitive and social development and in individual differences."

Great for academic study, but for practical use I'm with Jazz Rasool, the idea of stars and constellations both helping each other to find a place in time and space is elegant and a useful metaphor for when we are trying to make sense of where we fit into it and how we relate to others.

Jazz Rasool, who you have been briefly introduced to already, is an Astrophysicist with an interest in nuclear and quantum physics. He is a successful research scientist, speaker and transformational coach.[31] He brings together some interesting strands of science and he is fascinated by how we are all connected – especially through our energy levels. As well as being an intensely curious person who has a powerful Discovery drive (more on that later), it's his fascination with connection and collaboration that it's worth exploring here. When Jazz talked about collaboration, he explained to me that you first need to be able to collaborate with yourself. What an opening! He shared his ideas around three key things that we all need as human beings to cope, gain confidence, develop, and grow. The first is the need to be able to deal with being challenged. Secondly, you need the skill of reflection (so that you can learn the lessons from what has challenged you) and finally, you

---

[30.] SDT represents a broad framework for the study of human motivation and personality. SDT articulates a meta-theory for framing motivational studies, a formal theory that defines intrinsic and varied extrinsic sources of motivation, and a description of the respective roles of intrinsic and types of extrinsic motivation in cognitive and social development and in individual differences. Visit selfdeterminationtheory.org for more information.

[31.] You can find out more about Jazz Rasool at http://www.energydiamond.com

need the support of others. That is what gives you the confidence to keep challenging yourself and growing as a person.

When we started to discuss inclusion, Jazz had a very useful take-away on successful functioning relationships based on his three points, "take yourself back to when you were younger. You probably had friends who supported you. You probably had friends who challenged and stretched you, and maybe friends who were a mix of the two and helped you to reflect. The people who supported you, you probably liked because they were very similar to you, but their weaknesses were, unfortunately, the same as yours in many ways. They weren't the best people to learn from.

Then there were people with opposing characteristics to you, who've got strengths where you've got weaknesses. They're not necessarily people who you are going to like, but because they are different to you, they are great people to learn from – IF you can learn to appreciate each other's differences. Usually, we have friends from each category; friends that challenge us, friends that support us and friends that encourage us to reflect."

At this point, I'd ask you to take a moment and ask which one of those roles to you find yourself needing the most (challenge, support, reflection) and which of those roles do you most offer to other people around you in your circle of inclusion? If you are a leader, then it's a useful little model to use in your day-to-day interaction with people.

What Jazz discovered through years of coaching and mentoring was that often people's worst enemies were people who usually did the right thing at the wrong time! Those 'enemies' are the people who supported you when you need challenging, in other words, they collude with you, or they challenged you when you could have done with some support, or instead of helping you to reflect, they rushed you into action. They may have even had a tendency to keep you in reflection for too long, and you miss the right moment to take action. So much of our influence with others is timing dependent. I think that idea is so simple and yet so elegant. It demonstrates that leadership (and self-leadership) is more than just knowing what to do. A great deal of the art is knowing WHEN to do it.

How could that knowledge help you to become a better leader, a more trusted useful friend, or a more effective parent? Take a few moments to reflect on that instead of rushing to read the next paragraph ...

So many times, I've seen people at work rushing to include people in a group discussion or meeting when the person they have in their sights is in need of focus. They are trying to get in the zone because that's what flow people do, and an inclusion driven person thinks they are doing the right thing by including them in everything! This might be a seemingly <u>nice</u> thing to do, but it demonstrates a lack of understanding of getting into flow and the solitary, distraction-free nature of it. It's the right thing at the wrong moment. It's not the wrong action; it's the wrong timing!

Flow and inclusion often don't go together. Flow is a rather solitary experience whereas inclusion is never solitary.

There is a time for everything. Great leaders and highly effective people don't just know what to do, they know **when** to do it. That's something you can only develop with reflection. Great leaders learn that by becoming great observers of people (the skill you are developing by reading this book) and great students of their inner world. As Jazz would call it, you become your own best collaborator and know when to challenge, support, and reflect on your own actions. That's a massive part of becoming successful. It's not always about cramming new stuff into your brain, it's about organising what's already there and learning how to deal with all the information you already have but aren't always aware of.

Back to Jazz's insightful discoveries. He picks up once again on the topic of challenge, support, and reflection, noting that people in your circle who have a great sense of timing often either end up being your best friends, your most valued mentors or partner, as they are able to move effortlessly between challenging you, supporting you, and encouraging you to reflect, and they seem to have perfect timing about all three. These same basic forces shape our ability to manage ourselves too. You have to develop a sense of timing about when to challenge yourself, when to support yourself, and when to reflect on what's going on inside you and around you.

The Effects of Exclusion

When we don't get the support, connection, and affection we need, the effects can be life-changing. Late in 1989, the previously secretive state of Romania overturned its dictator, Nicolae Ceausescu. When the regime fell, the media entered, and the western world witnessed the horror of the effects of exclusion when journalists and activists revealed that over 100,000 children had been institutionalised. The shocking conditions that these abandoned children faced led to one of the most prominent scientific studies ever carried out on the effects that neglect has on brain development.

Run by Harvard scientists, the tests and their results were startling. When children are neglected and don't get the social connection that they need, their brains were physically smaller and had less electrical activity than a child raised in a non-institutional environment. It didn't stop there. These children had poor language skills, they struggled with emotional control, and had lower IQ's. The effects seemed to get more marked as they got older too. They were poor at problem-solving, had less capacity for memory and they scored lower on almost every test for advanced brain function. The emotional and physical connection isn't just nice to have. They are essential for human development. We really need connection. We need to be part of a tribe. We need to be included.

Nobel Prize-winning biologist Elizabeth Blackburn studies how our DNA affects how our cells age. She discovered that the people who suffer emotional neglect as children have more damage to their replicated DNA than people who have a positive support network. The physical chemistry at work inside their bodies is less robust, the more toxic and less trusting they have been brought up to be. Blackburn explained[32] "People who can't trust their neighbours and who don't feel safe in their neighbourhoods consistently have shorter telomeres.[33] So your home address matters for telomeres as well. On the flip side, tight-knit communities, being in a marriage long-term, and lifelong friendships even, all improve telomere maintenance.

Science has told us just how interconnected we all are and just how much relationships affect our long-term health. We will be digging into the power of Elizabeth's work and what drives her to do it (and how her discovery about pond scum can help you in surprising ways in a later chapter) but for now, what's worth taking note of is how interlinked all the different flames of motivation really are. We all need to be part of a tribe that makes us feel safe.

The great thing about how we express our need to be part of a tribe in the 21st century is that we don't need to be part of just one tribe. You are probably the member of several tribes: a work tribe, a family tribe, and fan of a sports team or rock band. Maybe you are active for a charity, on a board of volunteers or involved with your local school. I live in a little village in England and love being a member of my local village 'tribe' where every fourth Friday spent down at our village hall with a bring-your-own can of coke and a skittles game with the neighbours. It's an important part of my life where I get to re-connect with the community I'm a part of but don't otherwise get to spend much time with. I may be a part-time tribe member, but it's still very much part of what keeps me rooted to where I live and the people around me. That's the great thing about modern 'tribes'. Being a member of one of them doesn't exclude you from being a member or leader of another tribe somewhere else.

Each tribe has its own rituals, and those little rituals are often the ones that give structure and rhythm to our lives. Tribes and their little

---

32. I wasn't able to interview Elizabeth Blackburn and all information about her and her work has been extracted from her 2017 TED talk.
33. more about telomeres later but for now let's just say they are parts of your DNA that impact on your long-term health outcomes.

rituals matter. Those tribal roots run deeply through every single one of us. We need to belong. The bigger the tribe gets, the less connected to it we get, and the more we need tribal symbolism to take the place of individual relationships. That's the sort of symbolism we give to our national flags, our company colours and our regional heritage, and even our currency. Those things represent who we are and what we are attached to. They all tell us which tribe we belong to. They tell us when we are at home, when we can relax, and whom we can trust. Inclusion is a vital part of our culture, at home, at work and everywhere else.

7.7 Happy Workplaces Thrive on Inclusion

It's not just severe exclusion, like the cases in those shocking Romanian orphanages, that dents our ability to feel good. Even small and subtle exclusions can be a drain on our energy and emotions. Little things that we perceive as having the effect of pushing us towards the marginal edges of a social group can have a negative impact on our happiness, mental health and performance.

At work, simple things like being excluded from a meeting or being snubbed at the water cooler can cause serious problems. Once these feelings of being pushed away or left out start to stack up, the problem moves from being a personal one to becoming a more serious one for everyone at work. When people feel pushed out or ignored they tend to start withdrawing, backbiting, speculating and taking sides. In other words, the seeds are sown for the creation of a toxic working environment.

That's very difficult to reverse because once a cycle like that gets started everyone has their defences up. The good of the team takes on a lower importance than the self-preservation of the individuals involved. It's not surprising because by that stage people are often fighting to stay in the job, on the project, or in a position of importance. The next stage is that knowledge hoarding starts, gossip becomes the main information channel, and everyone starts (having) to look out for themselves. Those behaviours quickly become a habit and trust drops rapidly when that atmosphere becomes the cultural normality. Exclusion can be an expensive business indeed. You have probably experienced something like that yourself. Most people get their first taste of it at school, and sadly some people never get away from it at work either. Worse still, as that's the only thing they know, they take that toxicity with them wherever they go. That cultural toxicity is the exact opposite of the inclusion flame that most of us are looking for. But before we leap into judgement, it's worth considering this idea. What if the people leading the culture have never known any other way? Maybe it was like that in their family life. There are plenty of families where subtle manipulation, bullying and intimidation is the norm; even if it's hidden under the mask of it being 'done for your own good' . . .

What can we do about it? Simple: provide them with training, tools, and coaching to find a better way of operating in the world, so they start to have choices about how they respond to things and become better at managing their own emotions.

My executive assistant used to be a project manager for a large delivery company and she was located at one of the big depots. She recalled with vivid clarity how people were regularly bullied and intimidated. According to people she knows who still work there, it's still happening. If you didn't agree with the people in power, you were singled out. People had to become part of the main group, whether they liked it or not. That's forced inclusion: which you can sum up as 'our way or the highway' and it's a horrible working environment. There is no emotional buy-in at all. It's inclusion by blackmail. Do what you are told, and we will fight for you; don't do what you are told we will break your car windows! Yes, I'm being serious. That stuff really happens.

Consequently, not only do they have a reputation of being a workplace of last resort, but they have also lost most of the market share of the most valuable part of their business. There is less innovation there than at their competitors and the business always seems to be playing catch up. They started with the mother of all advantages, yet they have paid a heavy price for not focusing on inclusion. The culture of them and us has cost the company dearly and is still costing the employees to this day in emotional distress, a lousy working environment and a struggling business.

Exclusion is an expensive business. When trust is lost, everything slows down, and there is more friction at every step. It doesn't need to be that way.

Trust

Stephen M R Covey[34] has done a great deal of research on the effect of trust and how the principles apply to every relationship; inside companies, between companies and their customers and inside families. Covey's work[35] is a brilliant insight into both the positive impact of building a culture of trust and the negative impact of what happens when we don't.

The trouble with trust is that it's considered an intangible quality. One of the brilliant things that Covey did in his ground-breaking book *Speed of Trust* was to recognise and quantify what he described as 'The Economics of Trust'. The simple formula he devised is a little piece of genius with the capacity to change everything. His formula is:

- When Trust goes down the result is always that speed goes down and costs go up,
- When Trust goes up the result is always that speed goes up and costs go down.

For inclusion to be satisfying, long lasting, and beneficial in business terms it's not just the tribe that counts; it's tribe + trust that counts. There needs to be a high level of trust, and that only comes from

---

[34.] Son of the late author of The 7 Habits of Highly Effective People, Steven Covey.

[35.] *The Speed of Trust; The One Thing That Changes Everything*. Published by Simon and Schuster and copyright 2006 CoveyLink LLC.

high-quality relationships. You can have thousands of 'friends' on Facebook that you have never met. That's not a quality relationship; you probably wouldn't recognise these so-called 'friends' if they sat next to you on a train. I wouldn't mind taking a bet on the fact that some of your closest relationships aren't even present on social media at all.

In short, inclusion is about trust.

The Way People Want To Be Treated

There is an old maxim that we hear a lot, and that is to 'treat people as you would be treated yourself'. Henry Stewart,[36] CEO (and Chief Happiness Officer) of the IT and soft skills training company Happy.co.uk disagrees. I found that rather a surprise until Henry explained, "For good management, you need to understand that Joe is different from Fred who is different from Vanya. They've all got their own needs, and the worst management concept is to treat people as you want to be treated."

Henry knows that only too well. He has learned about his own talents and where he is naturally more and less effective on his roller-coaster of a journey through the world of business. His journey hasn't always been a happy one, hence his mission after a dreadful entry into entrepreneurial life to create happy workplaces and a company to make that happen.

Back in 1987 Henry and a small group of co-founders set up a radical Sunday newspaper. They raised 6.5 million pounds (that was a lot of money back in 1987!). You might think that was a great start until you discover that they lost the lot in 6 weeks because they created a truly unhappy workplace. Henry recalled, "… there were endless meetings, bickering, endless backbiting, nobody taking responsibility. Although it was 30 years ago, it still creeps me out to think about what we did there. I remember when I lost the newspaper I wrote in my diary I didn't think

---

[36.] great article by Henry here *https://happymanifesto.com/2017/11/23/business-schools-time-get-act-together*

I could ever be happy again". Henry left and went to work for a pensions advice company, "I only lasted 12 days. I decided that I would never work for anyone else again".

Henry set up Happy with the goal of making happy workplaces the norm instead of the exception. Henry still works directly with clients in his business from time to time, but he leaves the people management side to others, "I'm great at managing people like me, people who are expressive, communicative and full of ideas. I have a great time with them. I don't get analytical people and introverts. I don't get what motivates them, I don't get what they need, and I'm lousy at managing them. I am not a natural manager. So, I don't manage people. Throw me in an environment where there are 50 people and I'm in heaven, but there's total chaos! The one thing I teach entrepreneurs is that you don't have to do everything yourself. You don't have to do the managing, because if you are like most entrepreneurs, you are no good at it!"

Henry and I agreed on a key point instantly about Inclusion motivation. That there is one key thing that makes all the difference: kindness.

If you vow to be kind to someone and are confident that other people will be kind to you in return, you can start to share information again. Social bonds can begin to heal, and teams can form under the new rules of engagement. Trust can build and it all starts with being kind.

If your primary motivation is Inclusion, then even a mildly negative culture where people don't respect each other's feelings can cause levels of anxiety, and that's enough to affect their mental and physical wellbeing. If those same people have Expression drive as their next most powerful flame, then you are in real trouble. It's bad enough that these inclusion driven people don't feel happy as part of the team, but then if they express their feelings about the negative culture (as they see it), then their need to be heard will add a new level of damage to an already dysfunctional relationship. Bad feeling spreads very quickly by the people who are **most hurt by it.**

It's clear to see how Inclusion drive a powerful motivator and its opposite number, exclusion is a powerful de-motivator and the cause of many unhappy workplaces. Anywhere where tribes form the culture (clubs, schools, sports teams, universities, religious organisations, companies), there is a need for Inclusion drive to be capitalised on, and the risk of exclusion and the resulting bad feelings and behaviours to be carefully and actively managed.

If you want to keep the flame alight for inclusion based people, then building a culture of trust is everything. Henry sums it up beautifully, "What people don't like is being told what to do, micromanagement, and blame cultures. What they do like is, first of all, doing something they're good at, the freedom and trust to do it well, managers who coach them rather than tell them what to do and flexible working with no blame. I remember in the early days of Happy, one of the early employees wasn't doing so well and I remember deciding that I would really try for the next week to believe in her and to make it work. Things turned around. When I chatted with her a few months later I said, "there was a change wasn't there" and she said "Yes. You started believing in me".

That shows the power of believing in people. That lesson is something that Henry has carried into his daily life ever since. When I asked him what he believed in most strongly, he told me, "I fundamentally believe in people's potential and their goodness. Everyone is born into this world with immense intelligence, capability and love and some of us have difficulty seeing that sometimes. One thing people say about me is that I always start from a position of trust and believe that they will do a fantastic job. Trust is the core of everything."

What Henry describes has created a great working culture at Happy. People stay with the company and he has a dedicated client base. That's a far cry from his earlier experience at the newspaper that crashed and burned in the 80's. Henry and his team have created a great working culture, something he still gets truly fired up about every single working day.

7.7 Balance Inclusion and Reflection Time

We don't need to be part of a group all the time though. You will remember that one of the key things you need to turn up when you want to get into flow is focus, and it's not easy to focus when there are a lot of people and distractions around you.

From time to time we need some solitude. Sometimes extroverts find the idea of isolation a little scary and take the view that anyone sitting in solitude is lonely. That's really not the case, because loneliness and solitude are not the same things at all. If you don't get time to reflect and constantly surround yourself with other people there is a downside; there is not enough time and space to develop your own thoughts or to extract the value and wisdom from your own experiences. It takes emotional space to process experiences.

Even extroverts need a balance of socialising and solitude to become rounded individuals. Remember astrophysicist Jazz Rasool and his idea of the three things we need to develop: the right balance of challenge, support and reflection. He rightly points out that nobody can learn without reflecting on his or her experiences. There's an old adage about someone with years of experience as dressage coach David Pincus recently reminded me when I was struggling with something: "Do you have 20 years' experience Sophie or have you had the same 1 year of experience 20 years in a row?" Without reflection, we would all just keep having that 1-year of experience over and over again. We would all live in a sort of *Groundhog Day*.[37]

For people who don't reflect, they are probably baffled as to why they aren't more successful. That's what happens when you don't reflect; you can't learn very much. That's why downtime is so important. In a world where we are always connected, we need a digital holiday from time to time. Our devices eat into our reflection time. It's easier to view other people's lives than it is to reflect on our own sometimes. Reflection isn't

---

[37.] Brilliant film. If you want to see what makes people tick in one movie watch it! Bill Murray is genius.

always a comfortable thing to do, but I believe that it is essential for success, personal growth and the ability to adapt to change.

Inclusion motivated people still need solitude to develop thoughts and ideas, free from the influence of others. Developing your own identity has to come from inside you – and not from the outside of others.

Think back for a moment to the story of businessman Paul Dunn and the story of his dinner in Bangalore and consequences, the setting up of **Paul Dunn House.**

It's time to pick back up with Paul to tell the second half of the story. After seeing that photograph, his new destiny was about to unfold to him. As he told me "The universe is a very interesting place, you and I don't necessarily know how it works, we are just beneficiaries of it – but a few months later I was about to find out. I was mentoring on a program when a lady called Masami Sato came up with an idea that immediately excited everyone in the room. It was the start of the concept of Buy One Give One and right from the beginning I knew it was something special. Masami asked us to imagine what the world would be like it was full of giving. The idea took hold, we didn't know then how it was going to happen, but we knew we had to try. She challenged us to imagine what it would be like if, as a result of every business transaction, something great happened. What if, when someone bought a plasma tv, and that transaction gave someone who could not see the gift of sight (by being able to have a low-cost cataract operation), or if whenever someone bought a cup of expensive coffee a kid got access to clean water. I remember being blown away by the whole idea."

Three years later they had worked out how to do it and B1G1 was up and running, and co-founder Paul Dunn[38] became CEO. He had a bold

---

[38]. Paul had previously built several businesses to over $20M companies from scratch and his business growth programs for accountants are in use by over 156,000 professionals globally, so he knew all about getting results.

statement to make when we spoke, and I believe that it's the future of business: "Connection is what gives meaning and purpose to our lives. The thing we are in great danger of losing is a connection to ourselves. What more and more people understand is that connection is why we are here. You can think of that two ways: When we are connected, we have meaning and purpose – or that when we have meaning and purpose, we are connected. One more thing" he added, " it's not just about connection; it's about MOMENTS of connection."

When was the last time you really connected to your own hopes, dreams, and what you really love about life? Or to one of your colleagues and really meant it when you asked how they are today? When you can answer those questions positively, you are well on the way to becoming very successful indeed.

7.8 Team Sizes Count

For inclusion to be a powerful force, it's important to recognise what makes tribes and groups so special to us in the first place. When we're included in a tribe, we simply feel more connected, and connected people have better brain chemistry and feel better almost every aspect of their work and life. That's why married people tend to live longer. The connection to another human being lowers cortisol levels and generally improves health.[39]

So here are some useful thoughts about tribes and groups. For a tribe to exist you need 3 things; leaders, member/ followers, and outsiders. If there are no outsiders, by definition there are no members. We also expect other people to know and see that we are part of the tribe. We don't just need to belong; we need to demonstrate that we belong. We have dress codes, language and jargon that are unique to the tribe. We have rituals that mark out that we are part of something that only those in the 'know' are familiar with. The closeness of the experience and the

---

[39.] https://www.huffingtonpost.co.uk/entry/marriage-health-stress-levels_us_58a32c64e4b03df370da768c

feelings we get from being part of it play a large role in how much energy and effort we expend for the collective good of the group. Influence isn't about fancy techniques; it's about connecting with people. For influence to spread to other people in your tribe, they need to share their feelings, beliefs and experiences with other people. That's how movements grow. It's how companies with a strong culture, brand, and customer experience grow too. We'll look at some examples in a few moments, but for now, let's stay focused on the size and why it matters so much.

To connect with people effectively, the size of the tribe really does matter. Desmond Morris, the zoologist, researched this for his famous series of controversial anthropology books, first published back in the 60's. He talked of our friendship networks maxing out at around 100 to 150 people. I recall his research on that topic being fairly anecdotal, but it does make some sense. After all, how many names and personal details can one ordinary person remember? Isn't connection about being recognised? Morris' research suggested that most people had around 150 contacts in their phone books, which they knew well enough to call their close network; they are your personal 'tribe'.[40] Our personal networks overlap and that is how we cope with city life and stay connected. We have got used to walking past people we don't know without acknowledging their existence for purely practical reasons. As Morris pointed out, we have to walk past strangers in the street because we wouldn't have time to speak to everyone. It's the crossing over of our personal networks that have allowed people to develop what he called 'super-tribes'. Interestingly, Morris published his book in the late 1960's, almost 30 years before the first widely recognised social media websites started to take the world by storm. Although the first platform was much earlier,[41] Morris was still ahead of the curve in his thinking at that time.

[40.] https://www.webofstories.com/play/desmond.morris/25
[41.] https://en.wikipedia.org/wiki/Timeline_of_social_media

Morris isn't unique in terms of his beliefs about a rough effective size limit for coherent groups of people working as a unit. Some people have an instinct for it, and one of them is the well know businessman Sir Richard Branson.

In an interview for Entrepreneur Magazine,[42] Branson said, "Any company that has more than 250 people in a building is in danger of starting to become impersonal. In an ideal world, 150 people are the most that should be working in one building and in one organisation, so that everyone knows each other and knows their Christian names."

Branson instinctively understands that if people don't feel included in the company 'tribe', they don't bring the best of themselves to work. Not only that, they don't enjoy their work either. I believe one of the reasons for Branson's success is that one of his primary values is having fun, and he clearly has a great deal of fun by bringing people together and achieving something together that couldn't be accomplished alone. One of his former business ventures (and a very successful one at that) Virgin America ran an annual team building program called *Refresh* in the USA, a program that was compulsory to attend for all ranks of the business. Branson was convinced that the team ethos that Refresh created was one of the success factors that made the airline so special to both customers and staff. Although Virgin America has since been acquired by a rival airline (and Branson is somewhere around $750 million better off), he still talked about the family feeling of the business and how meaningful the relationships are, and just how intrinsically important it is to keep personal connections strong.

Inclusion has been a strong force in the Virgin Empire since the beginning. Branson recalls "In our record companies, when the business got slightly too big, I would get the deputy managing director, the deputy sales manager, and the deputy marketing manager and say, "You are now the managing director, sales manager and marketing manager of a new company. We'd split the company in two, and then when that

---

[42.] https://www.entrepreneur.com/article/223639

company got to a certain size, I'd do the same thing again." I remember reading that particular Branson philosophy back in the 90's when his first autobiography, *Losing My Virginity*, was published. It struck me back then how close the idea was to Desmond Morris' theory about maximum tribe sizes, and I often wondered if Branson had read the same book. It's either in his DNA to be sensitive to group dynamics or he has learned to be by paying attention. Either way, he has a track record of being able to sense when an organisation was getting too big and was starting to lose its founding culture and spirit.

Inclusion is an essential part of the cultural mix. The smoke signals that come from the Virgin Empire tells us that Inclusion is undoubtedly a primary motivator for its founder. When most other billionaires are locking themselves away behind walls and shielding themselves with a posse of security guards, Richard Branson turns his main home on Necker Island into a holiday home enjoyed by a combination of friends, family, and paying guests. I think that tells you most of what you need to know about the inclusion flame that energises him.

What about you? How important is being included (or reaching out and including others) to you?

Inclusion Motivation Fuels Social Justice

A good example of Inclusion Drive can be seen in people who are motivated to campaign for social justice. Think about social causes like B1G1. That's an inclusion project if ever there was one. In fact, the whole charitable sector depends on us all recognising inclusion as being an important thing. The same goes for politics, and the primary differences there are not whether we feel that other people should have access to the same level of opportunity. The main fault lines are just about the way we go about providing it (that's certainly the case in the UK anyway, I can't speak for politics in other countries who might have more fundamental dividing lines).

Our sense of fairness is something that is deeply ingrained in all of us. For some of us, Inclusion it's simply a part of our make-up. For others, it's what defines who they are and what they stand for. Just like DNA, it's not a question of if we have it or not, it's more a question of proportion and the unique relationship with the other motivating flames of flow, results, expression and discovery.

7.9 The Flame of The Activist

When I interviewed best-selling author[43] and adjunct professor at Duke University's Fuqua School of Business Dorie Clark, she didn't take long to tell me about her activist background.

"Even as a young kid, I had an activist mentality. I got fired up about a lot of social causes that were troubling to me. I remember that they didn't have kerbside pick-up recycling in my town. Even as an 8-year old, I was haranguing my mother to do the recycling. I would pick things out of the trash and yell at them! I was so mortified that recycling was a thing that one could do and that we didn't all do it. It was so wasteful. I wanted to do things differently".

That eagerness about making a difference has been a golden thread through Dorie's career, "As a professional now I love my work because the goal of the work that I do is to help people get their ideas heard. It's upsetting to me that there are many people out there who have something to offer the world, but they don't get to do that because they haven't learned how to break through the noise and promote themselves effectively. I want to break that process down and demystify it".

Dorie has moved from saving wasting materials to saving people from wasting their talent. Her outlet might have changed (she still cares about the environment of course, she just hasn't ended up being a full-time environmentalist), but her core patterns hold true. She still prevents waste and maximises opportunities for other people.

What Dorie was telling me was the secret of how to add real value, and if you can do that, you WILL be rewarded for it. If you can break things

---

[43.] Dorie's 3 books are all great reads; *Entrepreneurial You, Reinventing You and Stand Out**. *which was voted the #1 Leadership book for 2015 by Inc Magazine

down and demystify them for other people, you are going to be much more successful whatever field you are in. The more people you can successfully influence, the more successful you will be. Whether that's leading a team of people like the St. Tropez founder Judy Naake did, or whether you are influencing hundreds from the stage like Robert Craven does for companies. Your ability to codify something really well and deliver it to others will help you, whatever business or career you have. Successful people don't get the results by accident; they notice what works and what doesn't. They are also great at including and influencing others, like Warren Cass, best-selling author of the book *Influence*[44] knows the value of relationships and just how much they matter. Anyone who wants to make things happen, whether they are an activist, or a more traditional leader needs a network of people who are first to spread their message. Warren knows that an inclusion mentality is one of the most powerful tools you have to be successful yourself and to make change happen and he points out that "influence is affecting an outcome. It is about motivating a behavioural change or an action. It's about the impact you have on other people and their perceptions of you."

Warren is absolutely right. What's interesting is that people for whom inclusion is down the list of motivations often don't care too much about what other people think of them. The disgraced British business tycoon Philip Green is a good example. He hasn't appeared to be too worried about what people thought of him when he took hundreds of millions of pounds from his retail business, then sold it for £1 with a massive hole in the employee pension fund. With an estimated personal net worth of 3.8bn and the threat of having his knighthood taken away, there's a man who must be results driven first and foremost. I doubt any of his ex-employees feel very included right now and I suspect that not a single one of them have been invited onto Green's super-yacht down in Monaco.

[44.] *Influence – How to Raise Your Profile, Manage Your Reputation and Get Noticed* by Warren Cass. Published 2017 by Capstone (A Wiley Brand)

Thankfully not everyone driven by results takes it to the extreme like Philip Green did. Not being inclusion driven as the highest motivator can be a strength in its own way too. We all need people who are results driven in specific key leadership roles. That's because even the most caring person can't keep everyone happy all the time. A well-balanced leadership team will have a clear eye on results and a sense of inclusion as well who can balance the complex needs of real people. Leadership is an art, not a science after all and any art form involves a subtle balancing act of factors.

Inclusion Starts with You

Being able to accept and include others is a process because it's not natural to accept things that are radically different. Nature puts us on high alert for things that might threaten us. It's hardly surprising that we constantly have to over-ride our natural reactions. Before people can include others in a healthy way, it helps if they have a degree of self-confidence and a strong sense of who they are. That might, on first reading sound counterintuitive. After all isn't inclusion about bringing people together and not an internal thing? Well, yes. But you can't be a useful member of any group or team if the point of bringing a team together is purely so you can put more attention on yourself. Watch any reality TV program, and you will see the most self-assured people sitting quietly watching things play out and the insecure ones playing to the group to divert attention onto themselves.

I know lots of successful business people who have been through the journey of realising what's important and not so important to business success. Many of them started out because they wanted the freedom to be their own boss and the potential of unlimited financial upside. When they get to the point where they have all the money they need, they almost all gain a new insight; the car, the fancy house and the yacht doesn't have any appeal if people don't include you because of who you are. And how can you tell with all that cash floating around? At some point, most successful people that 'get it' and move on to become more personally or spiritually aware, they move into becoming more purpose-driven, more philanthropic or giving their wisdom to the next generation. Most people with any reasonable level of inclusion drive don't lock themselves away on super-yachts and get violent with reporters when they start asking difficult questions...

The only way to develop inclusion on a wider basis is to start with helping individuals, one at a time, to let go of their ego and to learn the skills required to help them to understand their own reactions, make better choices about how to manage themselves under pressure and to tap into their own personal power. People who start to control those internal developments become a delight to include in things and in turn, draw others towards them. They are our leaders of the future.

Then we are focused on inclusion for the right reasons and are driven to bring others along with us, and our personal power increases exponentially.

Bringing People together

Entrepreneur and spokeswoman for women in business, Valerie Dwyer[45] didn't have an easy start in life. Valerie started off being motivated by moving away from a difficult situation; she fell down several flights of stairs and was diagnosed as likely to be paralysed for life, "I willed my recovery. I was so grateful to be alive, but I had broken 3 vertebrae in my back. It was a miracle that my spinal cord wasn't damaged beyond repair. A million to one chance, my surgeon said. After that, I was driven to succeed and to make a difference. My quest became to help people make their own breakthroughs. My true path helping entrepreneurs achieve their vision took shape over time."

Valerie was instrumental in working with the UK Government to drive the growth women's businesses (including appointee to the Women's Enterprise Task force, Regional Chairwoman of the UK-wide Women's

---

[45.] Valerie is a Transformational Success Coach, Mentor, vision expert and professional speaker. Her website is https://www.mywonderfullifecoach.co.uk/

Ambassadors and Champion for Women's Enterprise, Equality and Diversity to pick out just a few of the things she has been a part of that have made an impact on people). She was also instrumental in setting up the £25M Aspire Fund and has even been to three Buckingham Palace garden parties for her services to women and enterprise.

Are you starting to see the pattern? All of Valerie's involvement has been in, and for, groups. She is a strategic thinker with an extraordinary ability to help people to believe in themselves and has the ear of many powerful people in Government. That influence at policymaker level has enabled her to make a huge impact on the lives of many people who she will never even meet. You will often find inclusion driven people like Valerie in ambassador type roles. If you are running a company, then inclusion-based people are likely to be your best advocates. A word to the wise though, if people with high levels of inclusion motivation *don't* get an outlet you can find that same motivation working against you, with gossiping at the water cooler and activism on the shop floor. Every flame creates a shadow ...

Parents, Mentors, and Bosses

In a fascinating interview with the business owner, podcast host, best-selling author and expert on reputation, Rob Brown,[46] Rob recalled his former career as a teacher. When he was teaching, he noticed that when it came to drive, the kids split into two groups.

The first group (and the majority of kids) needed motivation and encouragement to learn and do great work. The second (a minority of kids) wanted to do their very best; not because others expected it, but they expected great work **of** themselves and **for** themselves. These were intrinsically motivated kids who simply wanted to put their all into things and be the best they could be – just for the sake of doing their best. You might remember from earlier in the book, Rob's recollection about his felt tip pens and his early awareness that he was different.

[46.] https://therobbrown.com

When I asked Rob if he thought that his drive was nature or nurture, he was clear, "I wouldn't say it was nurture. There was just something in me that wanted to colour in between the lines. I can see how it would be a merger of both, with me it must be more nature because I wasn't brought up to be that way".

However, we don't really know what all the intrinsically motivated kids backgrounds were like, so science doesn't find it easy to measure. Maybe they were that way because of what happened to them in school, or before they ever went to school. I did a small survey[47] for this book that suggested that roughly half of the parents of the respondents[48] were driven, and the other half weren't considered driven by their offspring at all. There's clearly more going on than the example that gets shown to us at home when we are kids.

Rob Brown is no longer a teacher; he has taken his intrinsic motivation and applied it to a different business. Today he is a very successful speaker, coach and specialist in business relationships. His BD Academy helps top 100 accountancy firms to grow their sales and serve their customers better. Rob is as driven today, as he was when he was a kid.

I asked him if there was a moment that he could remember when he first became aware of his own drive. After his colouring book memory he also recalled a Physical Education teacher who had a big impact on him, (he later trained to be P.E teacher himself). "He would always give me an A-minus, and I would argue with him, 'but I couldn't put any more effort in P.E, so why are you giving me an A-minus?" he asked.

"Well if I give you an A, you've got nothing to aim for."

"That annoyed the crap out of me, but it would force me to continue to raise my standards, if I possibly could."

I believe today that what is being taught in schools will have little bearing on the jobs the kids are going to be doing in 10 or 15 years' time. In fact, most of the jobs that they will be doing haven't even been

---

47. Survey results available from www.sophiebennett.com/surveyresults
48. who considered themselves driven at a level of 70% or more.

invented yet. So, the content of school classes beyond basic skills like reading and writing are going to be largely irrelevant by the time these kids hit the workplace. But what hasn't changed, and is unlikely to change, is the impact that teachers have on them during their formative years. Many of the bosses we have early on in our careers can have similar levels of impact.

It's funny how there are things said almost in passing that will be remembered by the recipient of the comment for decades later. Even to the point where that single phrase can become a driver for life – even when the person who said it probably forgot about it by the time they had lunch. It's a valuable lesson in choosing your words carefully. You have more power to motivate (and if you act insensitively – accidentally crush) other people without realising it.

7.10 People Like Us

It's not enough to be included in any old group. Inclusion into something you don't care about won't cut the mustard. It needs to be something you care about. Something that you feel represents your ideas, beliefs or values. A group that you care about has to be one that you perceive as giving a fair deal to the tribe members. In fact, a group that you will contribute to yourself has to be even more than that. According to one of the worlds' leading experts on what influences us, we need to feel a sense of inclusion from other people who are very similar to us.

Professor of psychology, Dr Robert Cialdini introduced a 7th[49] principle of influence, 'unity'[50] that he describes as 'being about shared identities'.

[49.] His previous 6 principles from his original book *Persuasion* are repricocity, commitment/consistency, social proof, authority, liking, scarcity.

[50.] Details of Dr. Cialdini's work on the unity principle can be found in his more recent book *Pre-Suasion – A Revolutionary Way to Influence and Persuade* published by Random House Business

Cialdini cites an experiment that he designed with his team to help a hotel chain to influence the behaviour of their guests. If you have ever stayed at a hotel, I'm sure you will have seen the universal sign in the bathroom about re-using your towels and helping the planet in the process. It doesn't take a genius to work out that, even though the planet does benefit from one less blast of electricity and detergent used for washing your towels; it does benefit the hotel rather more than it benefits you. After all, you have paid good money to stay in that room and enjoy nice clean, white, fluffy towels. The deal is fundamentally one-sided. So here is what Cialdini goes on to describe in a keynote speech;[51] his team was asked to find out if changing the language on the signs would change the behaviour of the guests and here's what they discovered:

- If the signs asked people to re-use their towels to help the environment 38% of people hung up their towels.
- If the sign asked people to co-operate with the hotel, the re-use levels actually decreased! Cialdini believes that's because the hotel is not creating a genuine partnership. It's more of a one-sided deal in their favour.
- The 3rd sign told people that the majority of guests that stay in this hotel re-use their towels at least once during their stay. The result of that was what resulted in highest re-use rate.

That wasn't the end of the experiment though. What amplified that result was when Cialdini's team created a fourth sign that tapped into our inclusion flame. This was a sign that went beyond the principle of 'this is what most people do' and moved to a principle of 'this is what people like YOU do'. The results were startling.

The fourth sign said, "The majority of guests who stay in room 217 like you, re-use their towels at least once."

[51.] You can view the speech at https://www.influenceatwork.com/robert-cialdini-phd/presentations-keynotes-on-influence/

Using that sign, the hotels reported their best ever towel re-use rate. It proves just how much we are hardwired to be included as part of a group, especially a group of people who are like us. Even if they are not present. Inclusion and the opportunity to be part of something bigger than ourselves affects everything we do.

The Power of Recognition

You have already heard from many best-selling authors. We have also talked about Cialdini's principles of influence. So, you can see from all sides just what a powerful force being included and recognised has on our psyche.

There's another great way to put Inclusion drive to work; enter awards and go for the big prize. It is surprising just how few people enter awards and competitions. Maybe that's because that there is a fear of not winning them – or perhaps it's because you aren't that results-driven (we'll be getting to that shortly). But it's surprising what a little competition can do to bring people together. Having external recognition for the quality of your product or service can heap a big dollop of team spirit onto your company. It can do amazing things to bring people together. Someone who recognises this has built an incredible company based on that single idea and the power it has to fuel innovation.

Peter Diamandis, the famous Silicon Valley entrepreneur, is a big fan of prizes and the combination of team spirit and innovation that they can fire up. He started his business around the X-Prize and has gone on to build an incredible company based around our sense of teamwork combined with our natural competitive edge.

Think about the recognition that we give to people inside specialist industries. The big awards that we all hear about have a global reach; the Nobel Prize (awarded for physics, chemistry, literature, medicine, peace and economic science), The Academy Awards (Oscars), and The Pulitzer Prize (music, drama, journalism). What's interesting about these prizes is that much of the work done to achieve them isn't publicly recognised work until the winner gets the award. There's a big difference between prizes, awards, and competitions. Competitions may look the same on the surface, but they have a different dynamic.

Awards have a two-fold value. Firstly, there's the value to the people who win them (monetary reward, peer recognition, and public validation of what is often solitary effort), and a secondly there is value to the public who get find out about work they would not have otherwise heard about. They help to spread the word about new developments or exceptional achievements, plus they bring the winners into a unique circle of inclusion. That circle is shorthand for good, meaningful and useful work. Think about Oscar winners, Nobel Prize Winners etc. They provide a cachet to people inside the circle of inclusion, and recognition by the general public, who might not even understand the work that was done (that's often the case in the fields of science, medicine and technology) and yet the people who win the prizes are still respected by people outside their own field and direct sphere of influence.

So, prizes have much greater value than just the winners' purse. The spirit of shared striving can bring new life to tired teams, give them a shared goal of public inclusion and an additional personal purpose for a new, exciting or important goal.

So, what could you, or your company enter that could stimulate team spirit? I'll leave that one with you.

7.11 Learning Summary

So, what have we learned about Inclusion?

- Trust is the bedrock of Inclusion
- In an Inclusion driven environment people relax, thrive, and are capable of empathy
- We all need to be part of a group, but we don't all show it in the same way

- Kind rules. It's the one thing that can change everything and kick-start a culture of trust even when some damage has been done
- We evolved to work together. We are designed to collaborate
- We all need to learn to embrace difference, even if we don't always understand it
- Leaders touch a heart before they ask for a hand

7.12 Inclusion Black Belt Strategies

Black Belt Leaders ...

- Listen
- Are always on the look out for opportunities to bring a team together
- Stay focused, even when they are having a great time with other people
- Consciously work on improving their communication skills
- Consciously work on increasing their emotional intelligence
- Actively work on connecting with people and building relationships
- Don't wait to need something before they connect with people
- Give before they take from others
- Communicate often, so people know what's going on
- Don't wait to be asked what's going on. They stay ahead of the communication curve
- Care
- Manage their teams and relationships like Zen Masters

7.13 Why Inclusion Isn't Always Enough

So, if we all have an inclusion flame burning, isn't it the most powerful force for all of us? It's a fair question. The answer is simple; no, it isn't – at least not for everyone.

It's not that those who have other primary motivators are selfish; it's just that they have different ways of being part of the tribe and making a contribution to it.

Some people get their recognition because they get results that other people benefit from. Others get fired up by being in flow, and we get to marvel at their exploits and aim to model their achievements, some people who are fascinated by learning things and go on to make discoveries that change our lives while others write the songs and tell the stories that help us to connect with our emotions. We are all different, and that's a wonderful thing.

For some people there is something even more important than being part of the tribe. For some people, there is one thing that counts above all the others, and that thing is the ability to get RESULTS.

Chapter 8

Results Motivation

Success is never assured. It looks inevitable only after it is achieved.

Jeff Haden, The Motivation Myth[52]

8.1 Birds, Pumas and Pilots

The Magnus oil field in the North Sea was first discovered in 1974, a whopping 8,888 feet below the seabed. Named after a Viking saint, the massive find was going to bring hundreds of jobs and wealth to an economy that had been on its knees and was still in severe recession.

At the time British coal miners were out on strike, and the mood in the nation was black. Although it would be another nine years before oil production would eventually start and the field would begin pumping its black gold to shore, it was a triumphant moment for a nation that needed some good news. The men who would be pumping the oil to shore were destined to be transported by air to get to and from work. Getting people on and off the various rigs out in the Magnus field was going to be a big undertaking and one that was fraught with risk. Staff on the rigs worked a rota system, with several weeks at a time on the rig followed weeks on dry land. Rig work was a risky business, and it still is – with one of the most hazardous parts of the job being getting to and from work. Getting on and off an oil rig, miles away from land in

---

52. *The Motivation Myth – How High Achievers Really Set Themselves Up to Win.* Published by Penguin Random House 2018.

variable weather conditions is a challenge, carries high risk and many lives have been lost. There are dozens of souls out at sea who went out to make a better life for their families, but never actually made it home. The journey to the Magnus oil field consists of 99 miles of rough sea between you and the nearest UK land. It's even further from the main transport airport at Aberdeen, Scotland's oil capital. That means travelling by helicopter is the only practical way for rig workers to get from shore to rig and back again. Flying conditions over the North Sea can be treacherous, and helicopters are sensitive machines, which all adds up to a potentially volatile cocktail of hazards. The pilots who fly out to the rigs were highly experienced and had the skills to fly under some of the most testing conditions in civilian aviation. It takes nerves of steel and a great deal of skill to transport people on and off the rigs so, unsurprisingly, most of the pilots are former military pilots (or 'chopper boys' as they are often called).

On the 20th May 1987 a former RAF[53] pilot, Captain Peter Saxton was due to fly rig workers out for a shift change. Captain Saxton and his co-pilot Tony Wickes were to transport 17 passengers out to the Sedneth 701, a semi-submersible drilling rig stationed near the Magnus installation. The aircraft that day was an AS330 long-range Super Puma helicopter, described by Captain Saxton in his impeccable Queens English as, "Probably my favourite helicopter of all time, very powerful, very fast, very manoeuvrable. Built originally for military specifications but converted into a long-range offshore helicopter very well indeed." They would be travelling from Aberdeen via Sumburgh Airport (on the southern tip of the remote Shetland Islands) and out to the Sedneth.

The blade of the Super Puma goes around at 230 revolutions per minute, and the turret goes approximately two and a half times as fast as that, "You can't have anything come into contact with the rotor blades, otherwise you are in serious trouble. We [pilots] get very

---

[53.] Royal Air Force

nervous about birds, it just happens to be an irony that they are a craft that is flown a lot of the time very close to the ground. They're a singularly terrestrial way of aviating." Captain Saxton told me:

"It was a grey day, but thankfully it was a daylight flight". Captain Saxton had no idea what was to come when he took off that day. He picks up the story, "My ace card was my co-pilot Tony Wickes, one of the most experienced Super Puma pilots in the North Sea. He was a cool, left-brain sort of flyer and come the day you have to handle a pigs' breakfast, you couldn't have a better pilot sitting alongside you. We were flying towards a beacon on the Shetland Islands [navigation beacons used by pilots and air traffic control for navigation and tracking the position of aircraft]. When we were in flight, what we did was to put the radio compass to the nearest diversion. We could have tuned the radio into the Archers or Radio 4, but we didn't. We tuned it to the diversion just in case something happened."

Then suddenly, out of the blue, there was a huge bang followed by a massive vibration.

Something had gone drastically wrong. The Aircraft suddenly vibrated, yawed, and pitched up.

The commander of G-BKZH was suddenly facing the most feared helicopter emergency, a tail rotor failure in thick cloud over rough, very cold water. The aircraft, the crew and passengers were still 15 minutes flying time away from the nearest land. Saxton recalled that he was thinking at the time that the passengers must have been frightened half to death with the level of vibration. Things had fallen down in their cabin and to add to the confusion, the PA system had been blown out by the disturbance.

It was a heart-stopping moment he recalled, "I don't think we swore, which is very unusual. I thought that was worth a "Jesus Christ" of anybody's money, but we didn't do it."

Unbeknown to the crew, a tiny piece of aluminium about the size of the pair of spectacles had come loose and flown into the tail rotor blades. That small piece of metal had caused a potentially catastrophic amount of damage (Ironically, the offending tiny piece of metal had been placed there deliberately by the engineers).

"One minute you are relaxed and conserving your energy because it's going to be a long trip, and you want to be sharp and awake at the end of the day, then the next minute you have to spike up to meet the threat. That has to happen in such a way that it doesn't end up taking over and descending into panic. You get a big burst going into you; adrenaline, testosterone. Everything just whacks in, and within almost a split-second, the next problem you have is controlling that."

Saxton and Wickes got themselves under control very quickly indeed.

The next thing they had to attempt to do was get the helicopter under the same amount of control. That was not going to be so easy; a tail rotor failure is a potentially lethal event.

In the back of the chopper, the frightened rig workers had followed their emergency training impeccably. They had their dry suits on, their masks and waterproof gloves on and they were ready to ditch. What they didn't know (but Saxton and his co-pilot did), was that if they ditched in the sea and the helicopter turned over, the outcome would be catastrophic for everyone in the back. A quirk of the aircraft design at back then, was that if it turned upside down, there was no way that you could "get the damn doors off" in the passenger cabin. All the passengers would drown. The pilot doors had a different mechanism, so they would be able to get out.

"We didn't want to put the men in that position. So we abandoned the idea of ditching." Saxton recalled.

"It's a gamble when the decision is marginal. If it turned over, I wouldn't like to have that on my conscience. So we didn't have any searing dilemmas to deal with as far as I was concerned. We just knew we had to keep going. If it had been a calmer sea of about sea state three or four, we might have been tempted to put it down."

That thinking only took seconds, "Almost too fast to describe," Saxton told me.

"So, we go through the initial reaction and then immediately after, I got very, very busy and so did Tony." They had no idea at this point what had actually gone wrong, but Saxton remembers thinking "If this is a partial tail rotor failure, I've got to get the pressure off this aircraft". He talked me through the technical details of all the controls, levers, controls and measurements as if it were yesterday, then described what he was faced with next, "You have a whole batch of instruments in front of you. There are three of what we call master instruments (the spatial orientation instruments that show you whether you're pitched up, pitched down or rolled on one side or the other). I've got one as the captain of the aircraft; the co-pilot's got one because he needs to be able to fly. In a military aircraft that's because if one pilot gets shot, the other one can take over."

There is a third standby altitude indicator situated between the two pilots. This one is the final arbiter that gets brought into use if the readings on each pilots' instruments are in any doubt or if their instruments fail. At this point, the aircraft is still shaking violently, and they are still 35 nautical miles away from the nearest landing point.

The severe vibration is alarming, the sensation is bad enough, but what's worse is that it was causing the instruments to vibrate into a blur. The readings were telling Capt. Saxton that the helicopter was straight and level. His guts were telling him otherwise. At that moment, the term "flying by the seat of your pants" became very real. That was all he could trust …

"The worst moment [of the whole incident] was the rush of suspicion that both the main attitude director indicators (ADI's) had become unreliable. The instruments weren't agreeing with "what I felt in my backside" he told me, "What clinched it for me was that the airspeed was dropping off rapidly." To add to the crisis, the master instruments were giving the wrong readings. The standby instruments and the sensation from his seat were the only things giving the right signals – but he couldn't be certain.

He only had seconds to decide. He made the call; he chose to trust the standby instrument and his gut feeling – and go against his training (which was to follow the signals from the two matching controls) because those instruments were telling something that he just didn't believe. Saxton knew the consequences if he got it wrong; the helicopter would go into a vortex or start to spin violently out of control. It was a life or death decision.

It turned out to be the right call, and the aircraft started to stabilise a little, but they were still a long way from land. Wickes got out the checklist, and their military discipline and teamwork kicked in, "Load the lever – Lever loaded. Check Speeds. Six to seven. Check." They went through the checklist, "Check, check, check, checklist complete".

"Okay Tony, put out a May-Day call".

They moved the aircraft to a higher altitude to try and reduce the dreadful yawing motion partially caused by the turbulence being kicked up from the sea below them. That turbulence that could have brought the helicopter down at any moment, so the two pilots smoothed out the ride as best they could. The Super Puma drifted upwards. They were going to do their best to make it to the nearest runway that was on Unst Island 35 nautical miles away. They still had a long way to go. It must have been a terrifying experience for the passengers who had lost communication with the crew.

Eventually, the Scatsta runway came into sight. They were cleared for landing. The two pilots worked to prepare for an emergency procedure called a running landing (a way for landing a helicopter when it may not have the power or capacity to hover prior to landing). They were still in grave danger. If a helicopter rolls, the technical description that Saxton outlined for me was that "All hell breaks loose", but for the first time that day their luck changed. There was enough of a crosswind from the right to stop it turning over. They put the chopper down with a shimmy. Even the undercarriage didn't break as they had expected.

"The little darling stayed in one piece," Saxton recalled. "Tony stopped both engines. I don't think I told him to do that. He just did it anyway. We ordered the evacuation. We didn't need to tell them twice. The door came off like a cannonball and they were out. We took our time getting out of the aircraft. I switched off the electrics, looked around for signs of fire and closed everything off. We pulled out all of the documentation and that was it."

"I don't remember much after that. I don't remember the journey back to Aberdeen. I do remember an engineer telling me that he reckoned we only had a few minutes of flying time left, and I do remember thinking that a few minutes left is fine by me! I had time to reflect on the fact that for nineteen people, the day might have ended differently."

Pete Saxton was flying a helicopter again just nine days later and went on to work in civilian aviation, eventually running Heathrow terminal 4 for British Airways. "That flight in May 1987 does remain vivid. However, this does not mean it is regularly recalled, in fact, quite the opposite. I have rarely wanted to think about it, even less talk about it in the intervening years. The aftermath seemed to me to have been in one important respect unbalanced – unfair even – the credits were over-focused on me as the commander. True, the buck stops with the commander, but that by no means tells the whole story. It was a crew effort. We would not have walked away from something like that unless Tony and I had been trained to work together, Hand in glove, as a single unit. Which is what we did."

Peter Saxton still consults to the aviation industry and lectures on leadership today. He is a results guy through with a big pinch of inclusion thrown in. He went on to study and achieve a PhD in collaborative leadership.

That day in 1987, the required result was to land those men safely. It didn't matter how uncomfortable or unpleasant the process was going to be. The focus on the end goal had to be so clear that the way of executing the operation became less important than the final outcome. Go against training and the official procedure and just get the bird on the ground. There was a combination of instinct, pure skill, and emotional control that had to kick-in that day.

So, what does Peter's story tell us about being Results motivated? What did drive Captain Saxton to put the work in to become the kind of person who could get results like that under life or death pressure? Before we get to that, let's take things right back to basics.

8.2 Results Motivation Summary Table

RESULTS MOTIVATION

INDICATORS

Resilient. Winning matters. Cause and effect. Accountable. Systems focused. Goal-setter. Measurement-driven decisions. Destination-focused. Highly flexible (except about the end result!). Disciplined. Determined. Celebratory. Single-minded. Driven to be in control over circumstances. Be the best. Good at taking feedback, if it brings results faster. On a mission. Responsible. Compares. Measures. Visualises long-term outcome and takes short-term action.

FIRED UP BY

Competition. Growth. Measured progress towards a goal. Being recognised for their wins. Other results based people. Fast paced thinking. Fast paced anything! Consistent. Resilient. Being on time and on budget. Trophies and awards. Freedom to do it their way. Breaking records. Momentum. Clear milestones. Money. A degree of risk. Daring. Winning.

FLAME EXTINGUISHED BY

Excuses. People who reject personal accountability. Procrastination. Overly emotional responses - especially for losing. Slow starts. Moving goalposts. Lack of clarity. Lack of challenges. Not winning enough. No competition. Lack of opportunity to excel. Not being rewarded in line with their personal contribution. Fluffy stuff.

Keywords – Winner. Achievement. Recognised.

8.3 How Long-Lasting is Results Motivation?

Can external results be a driver for internal motivation? It's a good question. In his recent book *The Motivation Myth – How High Achievers Really Set Themselves Up to Win*[54], journalist Jeff Haden believes that very often, the answer is yes. Haden outlines his theory that "There is only one recipe of gaining motivation: success. If you want to keep making progress toward the things you hope to achieve, the key is to enjoy small, seemingly minor success – but on a regular basis."

Haden has a point, to an extent. Although the successes might inspire us, it's usually the failures and what we learn from them that bring us closer to the results we crave. If we have a natural inclination towards a particular feeling of success (especially one that's not easily measured externally by other people), then staying motivated is a given; even when we aren't technically succeeding at all.

For one person a measure of success may be being applauded by a group, for another, it's being alone on the top of a mountain peak knowing that in the competition between man and mountain – man won. But one thing is for sure, almost everyone likes to win. Even if we win doing things we don't like, the winning still feels good.

One of the main measurements that we tend to use as a yardstick in the West is money, and whether we like it or not, money has an impact on everything. How it's changed the world of sport is a good example. Away from the big-money sports like American football, soccer, base-ball, and ice hockey, there are subtle changes that have shifted entirely the dynamic of many other sports including minority sports like dres-sage.

Carl Hester MBE, Olympic gold medal dressage rider and coach, kindly agreed to be interviewed and shared his motivations. He told me how money has changed his sport and actually helped him take

---

[54.] published by Penguin Random House 2018.

responsibility. He reminded me that it's not possible to directly make a living from riding dressage horses – even if you are good enough to be a multiple Olympian. It's not an easy sport however elegant it might look when it's being done really well. Carl recounted how expectations of results have changed since our early days together on a dressage scholarship 30 years ago, "We all get an Olympic kit at every Olympics. I've done five Olympic Games now. In my first Olympics, the kit said, 'Winning is not important, taking part is.' That was the spirit of the Olympics. It is a huge privilege to take part, but actually, because of funding, it's not about just taking part anymore. Being at the top is one thing, but there are hundreds of people employed because of that now, to get us there and make sure we stay there." Lottery funding is allocated depending on medal success, so if the team does poorly the whole sport suffers when funding is reduced or withdrawn.

It shows just how even such an apparently privileged position carries so much leadership responsibility.

Sometimes, even if you just enjoy what you do, things change radically, and you then have a responsibility to get results. That changes things. It brings unexpected pressures, and that's not something people expect when they are aiming to get results.

Most people think that all their problems will go away when they become successful, yet often the reality is precisely the opposite. Success and money (they don't always go together, but the following applies to either or both) have a tendency to magnify things. That's why success without personal growth and the ability to change how you deal with responsibility can be a poisoned chalice.

Some people grow because of it, but some people crumble. If you really master something, sooner or later you will be expected to win.

Carl agreed "That first motto I learned might make you a nice person, but it doesn't make you a winner. Whereas now, five Olympics later, it's about performance and deliverance, not just taking part."

Carl got his first big break when the wealthy dressage patron Dr Wilfred Bechtolsheimer offered him a job. He rode and trained with

'Dr B' for three and a half years and in 1990 went to the World Championships, competed at the European Championships in 1991 and in 1992 rode in the Barcelona Olympics. He became the youngest British rider to ever compete in an Olympic games. He is now the coach, mentor and trainer of the current world record holder and trains a large percentage of our up and coming potential world-class riders and horses. I have witnessed first-hand his ability to grow into a leadership role and deliver against huge expectations of the team, lottery funding, UK sport and the passion of a nation. When you become a big winner, it's not just about you anymore. That's a very good reason to pay attention to personal development and leadership skills all the way through your career.

It's interesting to note that Carl didn't grow up with any great ambition. At age 19 he was still living on the tiny Channel Island of Sark that didn't even have cars on the roads. It took several years and many chance meetings and opportunities for Carl to develop his level of Results motivation. But there's more to do than just win the next medal. Carl effectively runs several businesses – he speaks, does training clinics all over the world, looks after owners and trade sponsors, uses his celebrity to raise money for charities, and is a polished media man too, "You can't make money riding horses, we work [on the horses] four days a week because we have to do other jobs," he reminded me.

When I asked him which part of the sport he now enjoys the most, he responded in a flash "Making enough money sustain this year after year[55]! In the beginning, it's about mastering your craft. It starts off with being completely absorbed in what they're doing (there's FLOW motivation right there!), that peels away and in time it becomes more about coaching and training people (there's INCLUSION motivation). I've had three phases in my life, which have all worked. One, under the

---

[55.] said while we were conducting the interview in his indoor riding area with the current Olympic champion training a new horse in front of us waiting for Carl to coach her.

structure of Dr B. The second one being motivated by myself and having to do that on my own and the third one, the last ten years, being motivated in pairs." Carl was referring to his rider/trainer/coach partnership with rider Charlotte Dujardin CBE, two-time Individual Olympic gold medallist, riding Carl's and Rowena Luard's horse Valegro.

Charlotte lives in the same village and still rides and trains with Carl and was training her new star in the background during the interview. The horses, the people and to a certain extent the medals, have given Carl so much satisfaction (and continue to do so) but it was when he talked about the process of growing up and taking responsibility for his success, and funding the place he now calls home that his body language spoke volumes. It seems that it was that second decade in the sport when he set up on his own and made the decision to become responsible financially that gives him a huge amount of satisfaction. "It's running two lives. And that was what keeps you motivated, you've got to enjoy the other part in order to make this bit work." He told me that other life has taken him all over the world and opened doors and opportunities that he could not have imagined on that little island of Sark all those years ago.

But we don't all get motivated by starting off doing things that we love. For some of us, it's quite the opposite. Business coach Michele Walsh[56] told me, "My mum lived through me, and she did it by making me learn to dance. She wanted to be a dancer herself, but she wasn't able to. It killed her inside. I remember when I was about 3 years old, every Wednesday was a horror-day for me. It was the day for my dance lesson, and I would cry from the minute I woke up right through being dragged across the park and onto two buses to go to the dance class. But I went on to dance and it gave me my first taste of success. I learned that when I worked hard, I won things. I started to win dance competitions. My mum used to take me to the toy shop and show me what I could

---

56. www.michelewalsh.com

have if I won the competition. I didn't love dancing, but I did love what it got for me."

That's a classic case of extrinsic motivation! But what's interesting is that it did spark the intrinsic motivation to win. Michele wasn't fired up by the dancing per se. It was a means to an end. You would expect a natural dancer to be high on both Flow and Expression drive, but remember that dancing was her mothers' passion, not hers. Michele loves helping people. She is high on Results drive too. Results count for her so much that it's hardly surprising that she ended up as a business coach. It combines her two primary motivations.

So where did her Results flame come from? When I asked her, she was definitive, "A belief was sown very early on that I'm a winner. My mum told me every single day that I was the best. I practised a lot. I worked really hard. I would do the moves over and over. That formed the basis of the belief that you can have anything you want if you are prepared to do what it takes to get it."

Here's the challenge for Results motivated people. Most other people aren't as fired up as you are until you find 'your people'. Up until that point, you are largely on your own. Getting results when the rest of the world is happy just ticking over can be quite a challenge, and results people often attract more than their fair share of naysayers. One of the big challenges is to stay motivated over an extended period. The key to that often turns out to be who you surround yourself with. It can be hard to accept that there are people out there who seem to take some sort of weird satisfaction from bringing you down, but you just have to find a way to cope with it and move forward anyway.

Michele had to do exactly that. Much later in her life, she owned and ran a successful company, but she almost broke herself physically and mentally doing it. She had been a boss of 30 people and responsible, but she knew that if she didn't close the business, it was going to kill her. She knew that she would lose almost everything except the roof over her head. She found herself going from running her own business, driving a smart Jaguar XK8 and wearing her Gucci sunglasses to finding herself in the queue at her local unemployment office.

A few weeks later, Michele was at a family event when a cousin sneered and asked her, "How does it feel now you are like the rest of us?" It spurred her on to get going again doing something more sustainable when she had recovered. She added, "The more adversity I get, the more successful I know I'm getting. When I was under the radar, a non-entity because I'd lost everything, nobody was judging me. I was invisible. But as soon as success starts to come back, other people are quick to judge you again. It can be hard. Especially when it's family, people who have the same blood running through your veins. That's why it's so important to surround yourself with positive people. You need an antidote."

She's right. It's crucial to find your tribe and build your support network. The more successful you get, the more you are going to need it – and if you do have a disaster, you won't be standing alone to deal with it. How much you fulfil your true potential does depend as much on the environments and networks you cultivate for yourself as it does on talent. In fact, many studies have shown that talent only takes you so far. What you really need to succeed is *Grit*.[57]

8.4 The Steel Man

Results drive can be a very powerful motivator. At dinner recently, I found myself sitting next to Bill Ford, a recently retired captain of industry. Bill is passionate about manufacturing and was previously a leader at major steel company in the UK. He had sold British steel all over the world and led business units that sustained employment in a sector that had been on the decline for years, something he is clearly still excited about.

[57.] Great book and fascinating studies. *Grit: The Power of Passion and Perseverance* by Angela Duckworth 2016. Published by Vermillion

He spoke with passion about two things: the people who worked in the business and his obsession with results, "The most important day of the month for me was results day. Everything revolved around that. I used to gather all the managers and we would pore over the numbers together." Bill made it his business to make sure that the whole business, including the men on the factory floor, got an update and found it utterly ridiculous that the rules around publicly traded companies made this so difficult. "How can you expect people to feel engaged to the business and connected to the company if they don't know what's going on," he asked me as he threw his hands in the air. Good point Bill. He is obviously a man who knew how to balance his results drive with inclusion drive, and that was probably one of the qualities that made him such a successful leader. He found his flames early in life and they still light him up forty years on.

Bill was responsible for the production of steel that employed thousands of people and is still a passionate advocate for British manufacturing. He might be retired, but he is still fired up by making things. He spoke passionately about the security and economic power that brings to people, their families and their communities and spoke with passion about how manufacturing needs more talent and how the future of it making things in Britain was dependent on attracting people with great leadership potential. As he was talking I could see his face changing, he literally lit up in front of my eyes. He got more animated than I had seen him before and his eyes sparkled. He was almost leaving his seat with excitement as he was telling me about the factories and the people in them.

So, what can we learn from Bill? I believe that his passion for communicating what was going on with his team and his deep commitment to keeping the whole workforce connected to the broader business goals is an excellent example of how communication is not an afterthought of successful leaders. It's a vital part of keeping the wider team all pulling in the same direction.

His ability to balance those often-contradictory motivations: results and inclusion is a hallmark of effective leadership. Encouraging continuous improvement of communication skills is a vital part of the education of all future leaders. To recognise the power of Inclusion motivation and to understand why it matters is the bedrock of what makes a great culture.

It's imperative to know what to say, when to say it and not always wait to be asked. People get twitchy long before they will have the courage to ask the question from someone ranked above them. If people start to get pushy and ask, then you have already waited too long before communicating something that's important to them.

8.5 Results are Easier than You Think

Years ago, before digital audio podcasts, MP4, and streaming radio I used to listen to audio tapes as I buzzed around the roads in my little Renault. My favourite motivational speech by far was by the American author and motivational speaker Brian Tracy. With his soft accent and the gift of a master storyteller, I was mesmerised. Brian's tale of crossing the Sahara Desert "one oil barrel at a time" was so compelling that I eventually wore the tape out. I never could have imagined that a couple of decades later I would interview him for this book. If you aren't familiar with Brian's work here is a short summary of his public work: over 86 books published, over 300 audio and video programs and live audiences of over 5 million people in more than 100 countries to date. So now you have Brian's background, it's time to share some of his wisdom directly from our interview together.[58]

Obviously one of the questions I asked him was how he stays so motivated. After all, he has achieved great financial success, way beyond the fundamental needs of his immediate family, so money for its own sake can't be the reason. His answer both amused me and revealed a simple truth:

[58.] To see exclusive video footage of the full interview, visit my website at www.sophiebennett.com and join the newsletter.

"I love what I do. Successful people organise their lives around doing what they enjoy. Why would you do it if you don't enjoy it? There's no deep motivation or purpose to it, it's just what I've always done; to decide on a particular goal and then take the first step. I wrote a book called *Get Started and Keep Going* because that really is the real secret to success and everything else is in between. Just decide what you want to accomplish and get started. Then, every-time you get a setback you just brush yourself off and keep going and until you achieve the goal."

Very few of us are that focused on results alone. We want to enjoy the process (flow) or contribute to others (inclusion), and we hope that doing those things will bring the results that we want. If we have convinced ourselves that success is hard, then there will be a tendency towards over complicating things and getting in our own way. If ever I'm going down that path and can feel myself on the road to complexity I refer back to Brian's work because he is the master of keeping things simple. When I asked him about his current motivation, he answered instantly, "I'm very focused on the moment. What needs to be done NOW to achieve the goal. NOW. Just focus on that. One step at a time."

So, despite Brian saying he wasn't motivated by a grand purpose, he is clearly motivated by getting results. After all, that's how you start any journey, with the first step. You get started and you keep going.

And that's exactly what Simon Chaplin did.

8.6 The Motivational Power of Meringues

We aren't all fuelled by dreams of Olympic glory, winning an Oscar or speaking to 5 million people over the course of our career. Sometimes, it's the little things that we want to have or achieve that make a big impression on us. For Simon Chaplin, it was the lure of raspberry meringue baskets that drove him to go into business. Yes, you read that right. It was all about the prospect of puddings.

When Simon was a child, his parents used to take him to a local restaurant called Springfield's. If his parents were paying he wasn't allowed pudding, but if his grandparents were there and picking up the bill, the ultimate treat was a raspberry meringue basket. His grandfather ran his own business and Simon made the connection between that and the ability to buy a raspberry meringue basket. His Grandfather Garner was a businessman who had choices. Naturally, as little boys do, Simon concluded that if he wanted an unlimited supply of meringues then needed to run his own business when he grew up. Simon now has a successful accountancy practice and other business interests and has built an income and a lifestyle that virtually guarantees an unlimited supply of puddings for the rest of his life.

It's no surprise that the golden thread through Simon's life has been getting results, "I can't think of an occasion where I got something without doing something in return for it when I was a boy – from tidying up to washing up or weeding the strawberry bed. I started work at my granddad's garage business by the time I was 9. I had a post office bank account very early and was able to buy my own car before I was even old enough to drive. I'm a firm believer that you have to earn something before you can have it. That belief has caused problems over the years, and I've had a few ideas I have had to let go of as I've become more successful. But as a starting point for anyone who wants success, it's a good belief to kick things off with."

Most results-driven people have a powerful understanding of cause and effect. You work process X and end up with result Y. If you don't get Y, change the process.

The law of cause and effect has had a powerful impact on Simon; secure an unlimited supply of sirloin steak and raspberry meringue baskets. Simon's primary business is accountancy, so no surprises there! It's all about balancing the books and keeping account of the scores on the doors. You don't get much more results driven than accountancy, though Simon was keen to remind me that accountancy is not about the maths, it's all about problem-solving.

To be a successful business owner, you need people skills too. That means that a level of inclusion drive needs to be present as well –

because no one can grow a business alone. It was no surprise to me that one of the other things that Simon does is to run mentoring groups for other businesses who want to learn more about cause and effect and breakthrough to the next level of success.

His need to share his success and methods with others is something else influenced by his grandparents who were deeply embedded in their community. Simon's work and business interest choices demonstrate a powerful combination of Results + Inclusion. People who outwardly seek to work in groups tend to have a high inclusion drive. Add a healthy dose of Discovery drive, and that's when things really take off. Discovery drive provides the fuel to ask great questions, and great questions expose the cause and effect that created the result. It's no surprise that people with this particular motivation DNA combination are often very successful in business and end up great coaches and mentors as well.

8.7 When Money No Longer Matters

The first impression of what a business is for is to make money. Money is the ultimate measurable result after all. That's why businesses may exist for many people, yet for some people, that's often a secondary benefit. Research shows that money is a transient motivator at best[59]; once people reach the point where their essentials are covered, any increase beyond and expected minimum has a marginal effect on performance.

In some cases, increased rewards can even have *reverse* performance improvements. Sounds crazy? Maybe, but there are plenty of studies to back up the idea that increasing external, tangible rewards (such as money) don't always improve motivation or bring greater or pleasure or satisfaction from performing the activity concerned. As Edward L Deci pointed out, performing seals in a zoo might wave their flippers

---

[59.] A book on this exact subject called *The Hidden Cost of Reward* by Mark Lepper and David Greene maybe old but still contains valuable research on the subject

for the public and be rewarded with a fish, but they don't wave their flippers when no one is watching. Just throwing more fish doesn't drive more behaviour. That leads to an interesting question about businessmen and businesswomen who don't need the money. Why do they do it, if money is the success criteria of a business but isn't the main factor for them?[60]

Let's find out. Jamie Borgeat, a business angel from the UK, sheds some light on that; "My drive has changed over the years. What really gets me going at the moment is the drive to get to see the potential of individuals. I can help them excel; help them develop their potential. That's it in a nutshell. I know it's cliché, but it's cliché for a reason. It's about people."

For the people he invests in, mentors and supports it's probably mostly about the results. After all, starting a business is not for the fainthearted, so you need to have a clear outcome in mind. Otherwise, why would you take on all that risk and stress? For the mentor however, it's about the people. That's a perfect balance.

Jamie gave some great insights that are universally useful for anyone who wants to be more successful.

"I'm just working with a company on an innovation. You can be really creative in some of the dullest areas. We have found a slice of excitement in the cleaning business! The appetite for this cleaning business has been huge. This little idea has become a massive marketable opportunity for a company. When you spot an opportunity, your own energy grows. It's catching. This warmth comes back at you, people miss that sometimes. When people are in an innovative process it's easy to be consumed by what you're doing and what you are trying to achieve – you miss the feedback. If you make sure you pick up on that, feel that warmth (or otherwise) it generates momentum."

---

[60] Beyond the money, my business provides my intellectual stimulation, a big chunk of my social life, a sense of accomplishment in several fields (speaking, connecting with amazing people, travel, personal growth and coloured paper clips and other cool stuff).

He also gets what Leadership author John C. Maxwell defines as one his Laws of Leadership: Jamie understands the power of momentum, "When you do things with exciting people and exciting projects, you don't work. I can't remember working for the last four years. I just get up in the morning and do things that I love to do. Once you get into your space, whatever that is, achievement is just a natural by-product. You will achieve, you will succeed, you will find a momentum, find a rhythm. I don't need holidays anymore."

Right at the end of the interview, just as we were about to say our goodbyes, Jamie said something simple yet profound. He was telling me about a business he was in the middle of buying out. He told me that he can give people "almost any of the resources they need, but until you can tell me exactly what you want, I can't help you", and he told me a story about a local business, "I was struggling to find the key to the owner of the business. It was a third generation business in a traditional craft area; bespoke joinery. It's a lovely little business full of tradition, character and charisma. A beautiful place, but the owner was struggling. He was a nervous wreck. He was sending everyone in the business nuts. He couldn't tell me what he wanted. He was going to lose the business if he didn't do something, but he didn't know where to start. I eventually said to him, "What if I help out and promise to never change the name of the company?" That was the key.

It turned out that his grandfather had started the company and it has been passed first to his father and then to him. He just wasn't equipped to run it and he openly admitted that, but he did love it. He just wanted to work in the business and enjoy the heritage, enjoy the work, keep employing his loyal team and do a great job for his customers.

"As soon as I said it, his body language changed. He visibly relaxed, and he found it easy to tell me what he really wanted. I felt the relief. It was palpable and a moment that allowed him to let go of the responsibility that he never asked for. He treasured the craftsmanship and the heritage."

For the struggling businessman, his motivation turned out to be about flow (the mastery and craftmanship of the carpentry) and inclusion (saving the jobs of his team and the heritage of the business). Financial results didn't matter enough to him until it came to the point he might lose the business. He didn't know what he wanted until someone else put the solution in front of him. By asking the right question, Jamie was able to save the company, save jobs and probably save the sanity and wellbeing of the founders' grandson. What a marvellous thing to be able to do. It wasn't just resources that saved it, it was resourcefulness.

One of the incredible people who contributed their experience to this book is Declan Loy, who at the time of writing is on his way to making a new Guinness World Record for the most triathlon races because of his 5-second rule. Declan's rule states

When you get a moment of inspiration, you have to take action in 5 seconds.

Now, triathlon is a very tough sport that's not for the faint-hearted. It involves cycling, open water swimming and running and athletes have to do all of these punishing tests one after another – without a break. Professional triathletes don't even stop for a wee during the race, I know that because it's a fact that a triathlete friend of mine kindly shared with me, and for some reason peeing down your own leg as a matter of routine is one of the strange facts that stuck with me. Anyway, back to Declan and his attempt at a triathlon world record. "When everyone told me I was mad, crazy and the whole idea was impossible, I knew I was onto a winner!" Declan told me with a glint in his eye.

It's a good example of how a clear goal can inspire people to do extraordinary things. Declan made his decision to break a record in 5 seconds and took action. He is now over halfway through the 23 Ironman races and has travelled around the world doing it, meeting some incredible people along the way. Without being results focused it is unlikely that this would ever have happened. It's no surprise that

Declan comes from a sales background – another results-driven activity. He's taken that same motivational flame and applied it to another aspect of his life.[61] There's the golden thread again.

8.9 The Deflating Results of Wasted Effort

When I asked Captain Saxton how he scored himself on a scale of 1-10 in terms of results drive, he scored himself a 10. Hardly surprising. And he went on to quantify what results meant in his mind. He said "it's about achievement, it's about self-perception, it's about ego (he added that he thought "a pinch of ego is a darn good thing!"), He added that getting great results is also a form of contribution.

"If you don't get the results, it's a lot of effort wasted, and not just about your efforts either. It is your responsibility as a leader because wasted effort also leads to disappointment for a team." He explained.

Waste also means that someone else's effort further up the line has been for no good either. Think about it; if you waste food by putting too much on your plate, there is a whole lot of wasted resource further up the chain that was for nothing (a farmer had to plant/feed, grow, nurture and harvest that food, then there was the fuel to transport it. The effort of the shelf stacker in the shops, supermarket shelf space to sell it etc., packaging material that had to be manufactured and disposed of – all for nothing). That's nowhere even close to a complete list of wasted resource and effort. That's a sobering thought. There's an important point about waste that Peter Saxton knows that the rest of us can learn from. It turns out that wasted effort sucks the lifeblood out of team spirit and depletes our personal motivation. There is a good deal of research that shows that when people know their effort has been wasted, it has a powerful downward pull on how we feel about our work.

[61.] Interestingly though, what keeps him going when things get tough during the record attempt is his inclusion flame; he is breaking the record and raising money for charity at the same time.

Inside Dan Ariely[62]'s book *Payoff* (based on his popular TED[63] talk), he digs deep into the psychology of wasted effort. Ariely designed a series of experiments to determine the effect of how much meaning we attach to our efforts and their resulting output. It turns out that when we know our effort is wasted, we are demotivated and quickly deflated. Ariely relates the true story of a large group of software engineers who had spent almost two years building a prototype of a new innovative product for the company they worked for. Just as the project was getting close to being ready for market testing, it was cancelled. After all the evenings and weekends working on the project that they could have spent with their kids, families and friends it was a crushing blow. What a waste! It didn't seem to matter that they had been paid for their time and effort. What mattered was only that now their work didn't matter anymore.

When we waste effort on something that's not needed or appreciated, it has a crushing effect on motivation. The example of the engineers in Ariely's book is an obvious example of it, but what about all those small pieces of wasted effort that we see in companies every day? Think about it. How many times do management ask people to do something, and days or weeks later the project gets quietly dropped because someone has a brighter shinier idea, or because they forget how important they thought it was when they first came up with it, or because resources run out or because something more urgent comes up. Every time that happens a little bit of meaning gets taken from our work. Over time, the flame dies a little. Sure, you still get paid, but as Ariely showed, that's not always the point is it?

Results driven people are hit particularly hard by waste. Because they are so Effort In-Result Out driven. When the effort goes in and the result doesn't come out it's particularly wounding. Their model of the world has just been badly messed with. They are prone to being

---

62. James B. Duke Professor of Behavioural Economics as Duke University.
63. If you haven't come across TED Talks yet, I highly recommend you Google them. The talks provide some of the most enlightening talks available online.

demotivated by a lack of clarity by any movement of the goalposts. Those goalposts might be targets that move arbitrarily or initiatives that get in the way of them getting results. It won't have escaped most people's notice that many people on successful sales teams have little patience for paperwork, soft skills training (unless it helps them close more sales) and anything that they consider isn't directly related to performance. If they can't quantify it, it doesn't count. It doesn't take many projects that go to waste or other initiatives that don't take off for these results-driven people to get demotivated and want to move on somewhere where they feel their talents or productivity isn't going to waste.

What we can learn from that is that it's important to be particularly thoughtful about new projects and ideas that we start and then don't finish when we have results people involved. Discovery-driven people are different; they expect some of the ideas to fail. For them, it's about testing and experimenting and discovering what works and what doesn't. Highly results driven people don't have time for that. They want to get the results. They don't want to experiment. They want to win and when they don't win you waste their time and energy. Even if you pay them, you are taking meaning away from them and diminishing the value of their contribution.

So next time you have a great idea, share it after careful consideration and be mindful that your creativity isn't misinterpreted by people. Especially if you are so good at coming up with new ideas that you are likely to be excited by another new one tomorrow. It's a sure-fire way of your creativity being misread by Results driven people around you. You can unwittingly build a reputation in their mind as someone who doesn't follow through!

Good leadership, as Captain Saxton reminded us, isn't just about doing the big things and not crashing the aircraft; it's about not wasting people's valuable effort and remembering to appreciate how much their work means to them. As a leader, the work isn't just about the output, it's about the person that created the output. It's worth remembering that. The work will be long gone but the person will still be there.

8.10 Leading Results Based People

Results Flame people have an intuitive understanding of the law of cause and effect. They believe that if they do X, they will achieve Y. It's a simple equation. Great work goes in, and great results come out. Input: Output.

It's probably the simplest of the flames to understand. It is no surprise that the .io domain suffix is massively popular in technology and results driven circles. Input-Output is the new cool. Surely, there must be a catch. If you just did X and got Y, then being an entrepreneur, a doctor, prize-winning salesperson should be as easy as painting by numbers and yet it's not. If X did = Y, we would all be able to put the right things in and get the right things out, but life doesn't always work that way.

That's why results-driven people have the same frustrations as the rest of us. They don't always get the results they want despite their best efforts. Working really hard doesn't always win you the gold medal or get you picked for the live shows on X-Factor. Input: Output just isn't a dead cert in the timescale that most people expect.

Time is a huge factor.

Results take time.

There are also lots of ways that people and processes get in their way and people motivated by results really don't like that at all. No one likes obstacles, but one of the strong points of genuinely results-driven people is that they are good at taking responsibility for their own performance and are prepared to drive through whatever obstacles other people put in their way. They don't just <u>want</u> the result. They want to OWN the result.

You don't get very far in the male-dominated and results-based environment that is the City of London if you don't have something about you and you aren't prepared to go after results. Sarah Sparks rose to the heady heights of Head of Financial Regulation for Goldman Sachs. She became an Executive Director of the firm, a challenging position in a company known for its aggressive and competitive culture. What happens when someone who isn't as results focused as people think, ends up in a high-pressure results-based environment? The answer is that they suffer. If you were to ask Sarah, she would be quick to tell you that it takes a heavy toll on your well-being and mental health. She now has a business that helps people re-balance themselves after being under high levels of pressure and coaching[64] executives in the banking sector. Unsurprisingly, Sarah revealed how her own results-based motivation had limits, even when she was younger, "When I was at school, I played squash for the county, my best friend played for the country ... I was happy to let them win if it meant that much to them. I didn't care about winning enough to lose friends over it."

Sarah was keen to tell me that people often imagine her as highly competitive, but impressions are often deceptive, "Throughout my Goldman Sachs days, people used to think of me as extraordinarily competitive and I'm really not. All I want to be is competitive with myself. I want to be the best I can be." She took me back to her university days, "When I was at university and thinking of applying for accountancy firms, my father was an accountant, and he wrote me a note saying there are only three firms to go for: Deloitte, Coopers and Lybrand, and Arthur Anderson. He added that Anderson's paid the best but wrote down that I'd never get in. That was it for me. That was the one. That was a huge motivator for me. I even remember sending in applications but not turning up for the interviews. I was only really interested in Arthur Anderson."

"You can be determined to be the best without doing it at the expense of other people. When you are doing a great job, it's all about you and the job – not about everyone else."

Being results driven is connected to the desire to create your own certainty. So, what do people who are lit up by getting results fire need to perform at their best and enjoy the work? That's simple, they need to

---

64. www.sarahsparks.com

know exactly what's expected of them and be given or allowed to develop the tools or process to get the result expected of them. After that, they just want to do the work and watch the results come in.

Results driven people instinctively understand what it takes to get the results by following a predictable process. They like clear goals, measurable outcomes and to know that behaviour A will always result in outcome B.

As long as the game stays fairly run, and the rules are clear and well-communicated Results driven people will find a way to get the results they have been set.

There's results drive inside all of us. The success of many recent inventions such as Fitbit, fitness apps, and weight loss apps prove that. They work brilliantly for Results driven people; there are clear goals, obvious steps to get where they want to go and a goal that's there for the record with no arguments. The Gamification of results helps everyone, but to highly Results driven people those measurements aren't just helpful, they are the whole point!

Results driven people need one simple thing. Clarity. They need to know precisely what is expected of them and what the benefits will be to them as a direct result of their efforts. Once again, although almost everyone benefits from clarity, to results motivated people it's not just a 'nice to have'; it's essential.

If you are leading results-driven people, then it's imperative that you communicate what is expected of them with total clarity. You need to be sure that you can articulate or quantify exactly what they need to deliver because they will probably ask you right at the get-go. And then leave them to get on with what you need them to do in their own way. Yet many managers don't do that. Instead, they lack clarity when they describe what they want, and then (because they weren't clear in the first place and the team interprets the brief incorrectly) they interfere, fiddle at the margins, and tweak the outcome and the incentives. If the team does well, the management raises the bar a little; they move the goal posts so that next time the goal is a bit more challenging. They up the targets over and over again. It works for a while because results-driven people love something to aim for, they love getting better, but it's only sustainable for a limited amount of time. If the goal posts keep moving it becomes frustrating for everyone, and it's totally crazy-making for a results driven person. They have a strong sense of fairness. Results are simple; you either get results or you don't.

So, what about the self-management strategies for results driven people? If you are results driven yourself, the research shows that you need to set clear goals for yourself. You could use a journal, a planner or something similar to stay accountable to yourself for setting clear milestones and documenting and tracking your goals and achievements.[65] Whether it's a sporting personal best, or a number of widgets created or sold; it's all about the result. The process is of little importance as long as the job gets done.

It's clean and simple. But of course, if you want results and you don't want to do everything yourself, then you need to get into Flow and include others. Without that, you can't leverage anything and increase your return on effort. Some results-based people will have a tendency to leverage systems and processes, and others; those who have high levels of inclusion in their motivation DNA, will leverage the efforts of other people. The systems people need to get into Flow to design their levers, the Inclusion people have massive potential as leaders of people who can deliver results.

The great thing about being highly results focused is that you have a natural tendency to keep things simple. It's a good way to spot results-based people. If they don't overcomplicate things that's a sure sign of it. It's because they aren't attached to the process, they are only attached to the outcome. They want results, and anything that slows that down (like unnecessary complexity) gets stripped away pretty quickly.

---

[65] I recommend *Check-In Strategy Journal – Your Daily Tracker for Business and Personal Development* by Robert Craven and Adam Harris. Published by Wiley 2017

Seasoned entrepreneurs are very often results-driven people. They have to be, or they don't stay in business. Jonathan Pfahl walked several different paths before he found the right one for him. He started off working for the investment bank Goldman Sachs then tried his hand at property. He joined a property mentoring group and did very well with the support he received, but felt that property wasn't the right vehicle for him. He realised that there was huge potential to use the same mentoring business model to help business owners though. He turned the mentoring idea into a business in the faster moving world of entrepreneurship. It was a smart move, but things weren't always plain sailing. It took time for him to realise that having a great idea and a great brand wasn't enough, because when a recession hit things got really tough. As he told me, "When I first started Rockstar, the strategy of doing big brand advertising and spending far too much money trying to get the brand in front of as many millions of people as possible, hoping that someone was interested, cost me a fortune." It was an expensive yet valuable lesson. It led to an important realisation that has become one of the core principles that now runs through the heart of his business, and is now a mantra that he and the team live by, "The only truth is the result. If every business lived by that, there would be a lot more success for many more people" Jonathan told me. It's one of the core ideas that drive all the mentoring in the business and keeps his own team focused on what they are there to do.

Former Olympic athlete and gold medal-winning rower Ben Hunt-Davis and the rowing team used a wholly results-based approach to move from not winning any races to turning the team around and taking the gold medal in Sydney in 2000. They had a filter that they used for every single decision, and it was nice and simple, they asked 'Will it Make the boat Go Faster? ™'[66]. It didn't matter if the decision was about what to have for breakfast or what they should wear, or when or how hard should they train. The filter was always the same. That simple idea

---

[66.] www.willitmaketheboatgofaster.com

turned into a winning strategy and Ben and took that simple idea and turned it into a winning business.

Sometimes people see results as tangible physical items. This businessman started his journey by being impressed by someone else's Rolls Royce. Paul Shoker, a successful investor and founder and group CEO of employee engagement company, Beyond 360,[67] is strongly driven by his inclusion flame, but he didn't start off that way. As many people do when they are young, Paul started by seeing the external trappings of someone else's success and decided that he wanted those things too. He came from a hardworking immigrant Indian family who arrived in Britain in 1953 and clearly remembers one of his early summer holiday jobs in a factory, "I used to see the factory owner drive into the site some mornings. He was a Punjabi Sikh guy who drove a Rolls Royce. It was a revelation to me that someone like that, someone like me, could own a factory and get rich in this country. My parents were professionals, but there weren't driven in the classic sense of the word – nor were my sisters, but I had seen what was possible if you wanted it badly enough and I wanted that too. I thought to myself that if he can do it, I can do it."

Money and being able to afford a luxury lifestyle was definitely a driver, and they are something that the media love to focus on. In Paul's case, the desire for riches was a helpful catalyst to get him to think beyond the boundaries of his upbringing. The irony is that when we were talking about what drives him, Paul was eager to talk about the strange things that happen when you become financially successful.

"When you make money, it's easy to attract money. It's that crazy tipping point where when you no longer need it, and it comes flooding towards you. It's not that you don't just have it as your primary focus anymore, it's that you actually can't push back the tide of people wanting to get some of your success."

[67.] www.beyond360.com

Paul was fired up enough to acquire the skills he needed to achieve his goals. It was in that moment of unexpectedly seeing an Asian driving an expensive car that his world changed, and his flame suddenly appeared. That moment affected his world forever. Skill by skill Paul built what he needed to get him where he wanted to go. He learned to sell when he was selling advertising in a student paper, (that business was eventually sold to Richard Branson for a healthy seven-figure sum and became *Virgin Student*). Next, he realised that he needed some formal management and leadership training, so he spent time with BT and Siemens. He got experience and leadership skills on someone else's payroll (if you remember, Judy Naake did the same when she first started selling beauty products). I did it when I first started writing professionally. I got a job in a company that trained business writers and stayed long enough to understand the structure of great information, and at the same time, I got paid to learn.

The next big transition for Paul was when he realised the potential of doing business in India after a holiday there. He had found his niche. He understood the people, loved the country and had an ideal mix of skills to weave his understanding of technology and markets together. "There was massive potential there, and I kicked off two successful apps that generated millions of dollars", Paul recalled. He has since become a specialist who runs and invests in technology firms and has a passion for mentoring young businesses and helping other companies to connect with their people. What started off as a venture to produce results after seeing a man driving a Rolls Royce has quietly transitioned over the years into a powerful Inclusion drive that helps other people fulfil their potential. In the process, he has produced some spectacular results.

Success never happens overnight, and lasting results rarely come overnight either. The difficult thing about long-term success is that the results sometimes don't happen quickly enough for the true connection between cause and effect to become obvious. That's where the Inclusion flame kicks in and becomes a vital element because success always involves relationships. It NEVER happens in a vacuum. Every interview

I conducted for this book, and every successful person I have ever interviewed has told me the same thing; you can't be successful on your own. Success is a team effort.

Even entrepreneurs who appear (from the outside) to have achieved a lot as a lone success story have someone who has their back. Sometimes it's a formal business partner who decides to stay out of the spotlight (Warren Buffet, the legendary investor, gets all the credit but Charlie Munger has been there since the start). Sometimes it's a parent or family mentor (for the late British publishing billionaire and poet Felix Dennis it was his mother who supported him unconditionally). Sometimes it's a spouse who is the voice of reason (Richard Branson's wife Joan has always been a voice of reason he frequently comments in his books). If you dig deep enough, there is almost always someone who is part of their inner circle of trust who never wavers. Success is always a team effort.

Going for measurable results is a great way to check that your strategy is taking you in the right direction, but long-term results take time to achieve, and the curves in the right road are only easy to spot when you look back.

Rockstar founder, Jonathan Pfahl, quickly realised that throwing big bucks at advertising wasn't going to get the results he wanted. He started to see that the longer-term strategy was less about throwing money at the challenge and more about connecting with people. Talk to him now about his proudest moment in business, and he won't be talking about the tangible results of the money, he'll probably tell you about watching as 300 young people arrived at a Rockstar black-tie award ceremony dinner with the Mayor of Liverpool opening the event. Now, you can't host a dinner like that without making money first, so you need it to get results – but always remember that the results come from relationships, not the other way around.

Yes, results are important. Yes, clarity brings success; but it is vital to understand that you can't get results on your own. To be truly successful you have to have the courage to step up and become a leader of people.

If you are truly passionate about getting results, then other people will want some of that energy from you, and your leadership will bring the results you want.

You can have everything you want in life if you help enough other people get what they want.

Zig Ziglar

When Results drive is super high, there are risks. That's especially true when someone's results are so important, and their inclusion drive very low (meaning their concern about the welfare of others and how much value they place on what they think), there's the potential for some less than desirable behaviours. What might be a positive combination on the athletics track is not going to be so helpful on Wall Street when you are dealing with other people's money.

Take the example of sales again. If you have super high results drive, but you are not connected to or don't care about the people you are selling to that has potential to give rise to less than ethical behaviour towards prospects and customers. Wall Street and boiler room scandals happen because the bankers and traders have high results drive and low inclusion drive. It's also not easy to be inclusion driven when the distance between the person and the result is so far apart. Bankers or a salesperson in one country affecting the lives of a single individual in another country is so distant that inclusion drive isn't part of the deal. Scammers don't care and aren't motivated by doing the right thing by other people.

For the sales teams who don't behave ethically, the systems are designed so that they get all of their inclusion needs by a feeling of a being part of a strong team (almost a substitute family) inside the company while anyone on the outside is fair game. That may be the potential dark side of Results drive, but it's important to fully acknowledge that to run a successful business, you need results focussed people – but not at the expense of the other motivations.

To make sure there is no danger of stereotyping here, it's worth noting that inclusion driven people can be great salespeople too. They just might need a solid process that they can follow that has been tested and proven because what they won't do so readily is to break rapport to make the sale. Results driven people won't have a problem with that but people who are very high on the inclusion scale might. They often make better relationship managers or account managers to increase sales from inside existing customers than they do out there hunting and closing new business. It's something to be aware of because it can have a significant effect on sales performance. I have coached and mentored many people over the years to improve their sales skills, and in my experience, the biggest barrier to making a sale is the willingness to break rapport for a moment while the prospective client decides whether they are going to proceed or not. Results based people don't mind this moment at all. In fact, they know it's the one that matters. Inclusion driven people struggle more at that point, they don't like to make the other person uncomfortable to get the result – and that often gets in the way of closing.

It's tempting to recruit results driven people when selling is the lifeblood of the business and that is what's required – *to a point*. The challenge is to keep inclusion flame burning just brightly enough so that the sales team really care about the customer. When you can do that the energy is better and the behaviours will be high integrity and results driven enough to bring in the numbers. It's a subtle balancing act.

8.11 Ways to Generate Better Results

This can be summed up in one word. Clarity.

If you are the type of person who likes more detail about what this means in practical terms, then here goes. If you want someone to achieve a measurable result, then you need to give them the numbers, or something equally quantifiable to aim for: medals, points, sales targets, customer satisfaction targets etc. There must be goals, they must be clear, and the steps to get there must be possible. The expected results need to be unambiguous, transparent and fair.

Author Brian Tracy said during his interview, "A major reason for procrastination and lack of motivation is vagueness, confusion, and fuzzy-mindedness about what you are trying to do and in what order and for what reason".

When you give results people clarity and they succeed, their energy in celebrating a win is infectious. Even if they don't share it with a team, you can feel the energy coming off them when they are reaching their milestones and goals. Sometimes to help results-driven people to get even better results just takes a little bit of imagination and understanding about what makes them tick. Companies like Fitbit and Under Armour who created step and exercise counters and calorie counting apps understand the power of results motivation. They have built businesses on it. I have friends who seem to spend more time studying their stats that they do either exercising or interacting with their partners! Personally, I might look at those numbers occasionally, but I don't run my life based on those numbers.

If you are strongly results motivated, then how you would react to the numbers would probably be a different story. Take Eric Jacobson for example. Eric was overweight; very overweight and decided to do something about it. Eric is a self-confessed tech-nerd (his words, not mine) and he started to use the statistics on an app[68] to track his calories. He lost 65lbs. The measurements element that he could geek out on combined with being able to connect cause and effect with such precision was the key to Eric's success.

A results driven person with his or her eyes firmly on a defined outcome finds it easier to prioritise, and that makes decisions a piece of cake. OK, maybe not the metaphor that Eric would choose with his new lifestyle, but you get the point.

[68.] http://blog.myfitnesspal.com/fast-food-addict-discovered-mindful-eating-lost-65-pounds/

As you can see, results aren't always about selling products or services. Gamification is a growing trend and a gift from above for results-based people who want to track, measure, compare and compete. I think it's surprising how little we take from the gaming industry and apply it to encouraging and rewarding behaviour in other scenarios. After all, the gaming companies spend millions on research to understand how to best appeal to the reward centres of the brain and keep people enjoying their product. A great game can be addictive. If we were to use that to make work as rewarding, then people would feel fired up rather than controlled by measurements. All we need to do is make the measurements part of the game rather than part of the monitoring strategy.

For example, how could you impact change on a sales team by gamifying their activities? I was at an HR conference recently and listened to a fascinating presentation about how one multi-national company was gamifying its sales performance. Instead of a traditional sales management system, they used a game type interface with badges, progress rewards and a fantasy journey with prizes for winning 'the game'. It had gone down a storm, and the increase in performance was better than the company had seen for several years.

8.12 Learning Summary

So, what have we learned about Results Motivation?

Black Belt Leaders Know That ...

- Clarity is everything
- They don't move the goal posts, it's a huge demotivator
- Results driven people understand cause and effect
- Results motivated people care about the things they can measure, and often discount things they can't
- Competition, comparison, league tables, points and tangibles count

- Keep one eye on the team, the strongest results driven person won't always be the best person to look after then
- Are careful about promoting the best performers without giving them people management skills first
- Support them with coaching or mentoring, just be aware that they aren't likely to ask for it because that suggests weakness and . . .
- Winners don't ask for help (they often think they don't need it) and they will struggle on before they admit defeat or failure
- Help results people to understand different ways of leveraging what they can do to get even better

Key Words: Clarity. Accountability. Responsibility

Chapter 9

Expression Motivation

9.1 Music to Your Ears

On Saturday, 7th November 1964, a little-known, 26-year-old actor was sitting in the green room at the Liverpool Playhouse Theatre just before his performance in the afternoon matinee. It was a cold and wet, miserable day in the North West of England. The Tokyo Olympics has closed a few days before and a young pop band called the Rolling Stones had just appeared on the Ed Sullivan show for the first time where they had caused quite a stir.

The actor was doodling around on the piano before going on stage. As he played out the tune in his head on the piano, someone walked into the room, "What's that? It's beautiful" the surprised listener asked. "Oh, I don't know, it's just something I'm making up, fiddling around with." The young actor replied. The listener was enchanted "It's beautiful. You should write it down." So he did. He captured the notes on paper and then locked the music away for almost 50 years. It lay there gathering dust, but even though the physical score was hidden away from the world, in the composer's mind, it stayed alive.

Then in the summer of 2011, it was time for the music to finally be heard. The stage was set at a grand palace in Vienna, Austria; the spiritual home of the Waltz. It was a stunning backdrop for the premiere of a brand new waltz, played from the home of Strauss. A flamboyant Dutchman was at the front of the stage dressed in a tailcoat and topped off by a flurry of curly hair and a charismatic smile. The composer himself (by now an ageing gentleman in his seventies) was sitting nervously in the audience with his wife. There was an expectant air of anticipation in the concert hall. You could almost cut the atmosphere with a knife as the curiosity of the audience peaked. It was time. The famed violin player and classical music impresario Andre Rieu stood to introduce the music – and its mystery composer.

It is quite a challenge to impress an audience in Austria with a new waltz. Rieu slipped into seemingly effortless German for the Viennese audience and recounted the story of how he came to be premiering the piece that night. People were spellbound. As any beautifully scripted mystery should be, the name of the composer was held right until the very end of Rieu's introduction.

The man who had written the piece was the Academy Award-winning actor, Sir Anthony Hopkins.

The camera panned to Hopkins and his wife who were sitting in the audience. The bright white light in the auditorium dimmed to a gentle red and the first few deep notes emerged from a single clarinet player.

The Dutchman smiled gently as he waved his baton in time with the tune. The music started slowly at first, and then within a few bars the melody emerged, and the melancholy sound started to lift as more and more instruments joined in. The light melody of a waltz finally revealed itself. Within a couple of minutes, feet were tapping, people were swaying, and the audience appeared lost in the joy of the music. The audience was enthralled and at the end of the waltz, the ordinarily refined classical music fans exploded into deafening applause. Hopkins took his bow. There was a rare hint of a tear in his eye and a smile that stretched from ear to ear. Interviewed later, Hopkins recalled the exact time, place and even the smell of the stale coffee that was in the air when his music came into being. He could remember every vivid little detail of the day he composed it.

Hopkins, as reserved as he might seem in interviews, clearly has a deep human desire to express and connect with emotion. He does it through art. He's not just an actor, we now know he is a composer too and apparently, he is also an accomplished painter.

So, what does this story reveal about the Expression drive? Well, Anthony Hopkins is an excellent example of somebody whose expression drive is so powerful that it runs through everything he does and has been the theme of his life. Artistic pursuits have been his job, his relaxation and his hobby. Expression is his golden thread and yet in interviews, he is reserved and describes himself as *not prone to shows of emotion.*

Hopkins demonstrates that people with a so-called 'artistic streak' have more than one way to express it. It's an inner drive that seemingly must come out in one form or another. Sometimes it comes out as playing music, sometimes by singing it or through drawing, painting, knitting, arts and crafts, sculpture or acting. By expressing the emotions of others on stage or screen an actor or actress can often keep their own personal feelings hidden yet express the human condition through the emotions of others.

Expressing to others is important to us. We are built to pick up on the subtlest emotional signals of others. Our creativity is driven by emotion too and even creativity has more power when it's shared; renowned psychologist Mihaly Csikszentmihalyi[69] famously commented, "Just as the sound of a tree crashing in the forest is unheard if nobody is there to hear it, so creative ideas vanish unless there is a receptive audience to record and implement them.[70]"

When you consider Anthony Hopkins' musical premiere in Vienna, it does make you wonder if that moment would have ever happened if someone hadn't walked into the green room at the very moment when Hopkins was playing the piano and persuaded him to capture his melody . . .

[69.] Csikszentmihalyi is often referred to as the founding father of the concept of Flow, and the first person to research what it actually is and what triggers it.

[70.] *Creativity. The psychology of discovery and invention* Harper Perennial Modern Classics. 2013. P6.

9.2 Expression Motivation Summary Table

EXPRESSION MOTIVATION

INDICATORS

Emotionally aware. Self-aware. Artistic. Poetic. Innovative. Experimental. Deep thinking. Values-driven. Connected to the heart. Aesthetics REALLY matter. Expressive communicator. Values emotional connection. Emotionally intelligent. Sensitive to criticism. Picks up on energies of others. Tendency to take things to heart. Fiercely loyal. High empathy. Presence. Enjoys artistic pursuits and hobbies. Sensory.

FIRED UP BY

Starting new things. Colour. Emotional connection. Understanding others. Socialising. Expressing themselves. Beauty. Wellbeing. Meaning. Purpose. Listen, feel, act. Service. Appreciation. Music. Stories. Craftsmanship. Nature. Perfect timing. Self-development. Experimenting with ideas. Thinking deeply about things. Spiritual progression. TRUTH. TRUST

FLAME EXTINGUISHED BY

Not having a voice. Not being listened to. Drabness. Emotional flatness. People who don't care. Poor design. Number crunching. Anything done without heart. Results only focus. Lack of variety. Data. Lack of recognition. Lack of honesty.

Most important words – Trust. Beauty. Humanity.

9.3 Bringing Ideas to Life

Stories have had the power to transfix us for millennia. It's the way we have shared knowledge and passed down our culture and experience. We are storytellers by nature. For some of us, that connection with our emotions is our most significant driver.

One of the most potent storytelling platforms for true stories is the TED[71] talk movement. Taking an idea and putting it into a format where it becomes 'an idea worth spreading' (TED's strap-line) takes a great deal of skill and a deep understanding of the emotional reactions of an audience. Unsurprisingly, there are great coaches behind the scenes who help people extract those moments and help the speakers craft their stories. One coach who deeply understands the power of a great story is Dutch TEDx speaker coach Nienke Van Bezooijen.

Nienke has a gift for finding that little golden thread inside someone's story and weaving it into something magical. There's an art to that. In some ways, storytelling is the ultimate Expression skill. So where does that flame come from? As with a seemingly large proportion of people who become successful in the arts, Nienke had a difficult time as a child and a teenager.

"I've always been different. I was bullied a lot, even from kindergarten, but in junior school, I realised that people listened to my ideas, so from time to time I got a reprieve from the bullies. It wasn't easy, as I had to look after my mum who wasn't well. At 17 I got a virus and ended up paralysed right down my left side. It affected my eyes too, so I couldn't even read. It took 6 days before the doctors realised that it was something serious." (it was Guillain-Barre disease and thankfully Nienke gradually recovered). The signs of Expression drive are everywhere; Nienke danced as a young woman, wrote poetry, painted, and sang. In her early years, she was considered for a music scholarship and these days she sings in a quartet as a hobby. (Singing as part of a group

---

[71.] www. TED.com

suggests a strong Inclusion drive and inclusion people prefer not to do things solo). So, I dug deeper into her artistic side and asked her what she loved about dancing, "It's the coordination and movement as one with another person. Bingo. There it was again. So, I dug a little more about her (apparently) eclectic career. It turns out that she spent time as an au pair in England and later became a nurse (Inclusion drive again).

The content might have changed (music/au pair/nursing), but the theme has always been the same: nurturing families and groups (like quartets of singers) who are small and tight-knit and preferably in an artistic setting. Now Nienke builds and nurtures a network of entrepreneurial woman as an ambassador for women leaders, and on top of that she runs her core speaker coaching business[72] Presentation-Master. As is so often the case, the content and job might change – but the theme is there like a golden thread running through life. Nienke's Expression and Inclusion flames have been her golden thread.

Motivation never runs just one-way though. It's much easier to de-motivate someone than it is to motivate them. Maybe that's why schools and organisations do it so well! So how would you de-motivate someone like Nienke? Simple, just restrict her creativity and isolate her. Asking her to be a star in an empty universe would be a disaster. Yet every day, in corporate life we do that to people.

HR is a classic case of this. Last year I exhibited at a major HR strategy conference and unsurprisingly had conversations with lots of HR professionals. They talked about the people in their organisations and why they were in HR and yet when I asked what they did in their day job they told me that they were involved in data analytics, performance metrics on spreadsheets and absence management systems! That's fine if you are a data geek (and geeks, we need you... that term is a compliment), but it's not okay if you are one of the people who went into to HR because you were drawn to the word HUMAN. Maybe there should be a new department called Data About Humans who could deal with

---

[72.] http://presentation-master.com

the data and the metrics driven and another department called the People Who Care About People Dept. who could do all the unquantifiable stuff.

Just imagine how cool it would be if instead of corporate life sapping so many souls, it enhanced them instead.

So where does our early motivation come from? For some of us it's a reaction to negative experiences and to not having enough (you are going to hear a story involving late nights and stealing potatoes later on that beautifully illustrates the long-term effects of our early experiences). For others, it's a blossoming under the encouragement of someone who we admire.

Nienke's grandfather always believed in her. He struggled after the war to feed his family (starvation was rife in the Netherlands in the immediate post-war period) and he was determined to work his way to a better life. "My grandfather never studied for hours, but he did it every day." Yet more proof (if you need any more!) that you don't need to be spectacular, just dedicated. He trained as an accountant and became one of the founders of KPMG.

Paul Rees, a successful business coach, didn't start off a high performer. In his own words, he was "slow at school." Paul was dyslexic and for a long time, his condition went undiagnosed. "I went to a Welsh speaking school, but when I left school things took off for me. Everything I did, I always did to the max. Paul worked for a furniture manufacturing business for over 15 years where he started as a labourer and worked his way up. He recalls always playing full out, "If I was tasked to fill a skip I didn't do as little as I could get away with like lots of guys would, I did the opposite. I always did as MUCH as possible. I went from being a services boy on the shop floor to a role where I worked with the directors. It wasn't a small company; it was one of the biggest in Europe at the time. My work ethic got me there. I wanted to be a success."

He's now an executive coach and has studied what pushes people to succeed and what gets in the way of success. He has an interesting perspective on them and clearly gets in flow himself by understanding the emotions that fuel us and those that stop us. He has recognised that it's his expression drive that gives him satisfaction and is where he is best positioned to help others. He has strong opinions on what drives us, "When we are driven from a young age, I believe that it's because we are looking for recognition. As entrepreneurs we get our recognition from our projects, and when we get a success we feel great about it, but it soon wears off and we need another project again. Most entrepreneurs I work with come from that place. That drive for recognition and working hard and achieving goals becomes a way of life."

Our interview quickly came back to the idea of drive starting from a need to be recognised and it certainly did provide some fascinating insights. Paul certainly challenged my thinking when he said, "Grit and determination come from hurt and doubt. The reason we have determination is that we are running from doubt."

It's doubt and uncertainty that causes worry for most of us. No one wants an uncertain future, and yet if Paul is right (and I suspect he is to a certain extent), then it's that very avoidance of doubt that is the 'grit in the oyster' that makes most of our successes possible. What a perspective! I don't think there are many entrepreneurs who would question the idea that the reason they want more money is that they want to hedge against uncertainty in their future life. That is, to a point, the same concept as running away from doubt. Paul might just be onto something quite profound with his ideas – even if many entrepreneurs don't find the language around it tolerable.

Paul continued, "The reason we are running away from doubt is that we are running away from disappointment. We get determined to make something successful, so we don't have to feel that disappointment again. Those who get successful easily are those who understand disappointment."

People who have high levels of Expression drive feel their emotions very strongly. If, like Anthony Hopkins, they aren't prone to showing strong displays of personal emotion they will find a way through their artistic outlet to express them. Just because they don't show emotion does not mean they aren't emotional people! As they progress in their personal development and mental maturity, they just keep getting better and processing those emotions and turning them into a help instead of them being a hindrance.

9.4 Where Does Expression Drive Fit?

Expression drive creates a highly creative type of energy. Suzy Walker, editor-in-chief of Psychologies[73] Magazine, discovered at the age of 14 that it was writing and creativity that lit up her world. During our conversation about motivation, she had a great question that she has always used as a decision making filter, "Does it make your heart leap or sink?"

As Suzy points out what makes your heart leap isn't necessarily what you are good at. You might be good at admin, but if it doesn't make your heart leap then it's not going to make you happy. We all have to do things that don't make our hearts sing from time to time, but I believe that the continued effort of the search for that unique thing that makes you both happy and productive, is well worth it. Some of us know from early on what we love, for others, it comes much later. Suzy got a sharp jolt early in life that made her determined not to waste a single minute; she lost both her parents to cancer when she was a teenager, "At a very early age I learned that life can end very quickly. So how do I want to spend my life?"

That simple question – 'does it make your heart leap or heart sing' helped her find her path in life, "I wanted to write. I've always wanted to write. I found out when I was 14 that I wanted to write. I won a short story competition. I started to send out ideas to Reader's Digest when I was 14 and got very proud of my first rejection letter. I had no idea then how I was going to make a career out of writing."

---

73. www.psychologies.co.uk – a women's personal development magazine about personal potential and wellbeing.

So she did what creative people do when they want something. She tried things until she found what worked. She came out of university and got a job at a newspaper, The Leeds Weekly News. It wasn't a writing job; she was in sales selling advertising space. She quickly realised she was on the wrong side of the fence, but it was a way in. After failed attempts at moving over, she realised she was going to have to retrain to be a journalist and applied for a three-month course in journalism but was rejected. "They told me my standard of English wasn't high enough to get on the course", but she didn't take no for an answer, applied again and got in, "Within three months, I'd become a journalist."

At this point, it's worth mentioning that journalism per se isn't necessarily <u>always</u> a job where expression motivation is the biggest driver. For example, if you think about what it takes to be an investigative journalist, it's more about the search, so they have to be really curious. It's not so much about art as it is about truth. For deep investigative work to uncover corruption, crime, or political wrongdoing, I would say that there needs to be a high level of discovery drive. It's about the search itself rather than the beauty of the words. That type of journalism is about discovering the truth and bringing facts that people don't want discovered into the light.

There are different drives behind different types of journalism. Daily newspaper journalism is deadline driven and much faster paced. In that environment, you might be writing or creating news content, but the pressures and the level detail required is entirely different. For that to be appealing, you need a high level of results drive. Results driven people often thrive under pressure and the thinnest of time margins. That result of a page published just in time would give a Results driven person a considerable buzz. If that's not your style, you would quickly burn out.

The type of journalism Suzy does (highly creative work, beautifully delivered, aesthetically pleasing and delving deep into our emotional, physical and spiritual well-being) is an emotionally driven activity. You need to be the type of person who never runs out of ideas to produce work like that and that's Suzy's natural strong point. "I'm really good at ideas. I have a million ideas. I have always found coming up with ideas really, really easy. What I've also found out is I'm quite determined. I was on a course with lots of much more talented people than I was. But what they couldn't bear is to be rejected. I got rejected all the time. You just become better at dealing with rejection. Being rejected from an article might be kind of devastating for somebody else, but for me, it was like, yeah whatever. Move on. Next. And because also I had so many other ideas, it didn't matter if one idea was rejected because I had 10 more. I just used to pitch, pitch, pitch, pitch, pitch. All the time. It was a numbers game. Sometimes I'd be pitching 50 ideas in a week, and I'd get one acceptance. As I learnt how it worked a bit more, then I would get a better conversion rate. But because I had so many ideas, it didn't matter because I could always do it. And then slowly I built up a business of being able to work for five or six people who liked my ideas, and I was good at those ideas. Early on I became very resilient." Now Suzy has a team of journalists working on the magazine, so she doesn't have to do all the writing anymore, but producing it still requires huge creative energy "the magazine will probably have about a thousand different pieces of information going into it every month," she told me, "and probably 2,000 to 3,000 creative hits every month of headlines, subs [headlines] and they all have to be read. So there's so much creative stimulation. That just lights me up. I feel it's almost my perfect job."

It's a very opportune moment to talk about the combination of the motivational flames.

Suzy told me about what how she really became effective when she started to become more results driven. She said that she used to do most things based on intuition and feel, but as editor, there were the numbers to deal with. It was new territory. It helped her grow, "I'm getting a lot smarter and quite creative about how I'm using those numbers. What's happening to those numbers there? What on Earth is happening there? It's exhilarating. It's the first time I've ever been excited by numbers, but you notice things." That's a sure sign that a new motivational flame has been lit. She was really lit up by it, "Probably the results piece is the place where I've been least interested cause it's all about my gut feel versus the actual reality of stuff, but now it's getting really interesting to explore."

As with most successful people Suzy has her paramount driving forces, the ones that come naturally. Over time though, what happens if we keep progressing with our own personal development (that means we keep learning and consciously developing our understanding and our skills so that we don't get stuck), is that we keep adding new layers to ourselves. When we develop some competence and start to grow in confidence, we begin to enjoy the experience more and more. That, in turn, leads to higher motivation in that area.

Suzy started off with a million ideas and wanted to write. She was fascinated by people, so ended up in a place where the work was all about our inner journey and outer success. There was always a level of discovery drive – journalists of every sort need a healthy dose of that. More recently she has learned about understanding and using the numbers to drive growth and it has turned into a new motivation for her. She's now seeing the purpose of the figures, and she is using them to make things better and make the magazine more successful.

Earlier in the book, you met Carl Hester, the Olympic dressage rider. It's worth just making the connection between the sport of dressage and Expression drive because there is a strong link there too. Dressage is a subjective sport. It has technical marks of course, or it wouldn't be a sport, but the superstars turn the movements into an art. A bit like the sport of ice skating, the medals are decided on the beauty and emotion of the final performance to music. The bond between any human and animal working together in perfect harmony creates a level of flow and Carl told me that even as high pressure as an Olympic Games, that "once you're on your horse, all that pressure goes away. Once I'm on the horse, everything is gone. Job in hand, I know what to do."

I know as a rider that you can't connect properly and communicate effectively if you aren't listening to the horse underneath you. Communication and empathy are deeply rooted in our emotions. We are emotional beings and we can't just deny that because we are at work. I believe our next generation of workers and where the world of work will have to go is to help people to find what they love to do. We will have robots and artificial intelligence to things that don't require any emotion. To have sustainable change, we need to connect more deeply with what we do.

Is There a Place for Music in the Workplace?

Think about beautiful music, it connects into your soul and speaks to you. You don't need a composer to tell you if the music is upbeat, sad or haunting; you just know. You don't need to know if a painting is whimsical or inspiring, you just know. You don't need someone to tell you if a view is a beautiful landscape that takes your breath away or if it's an ugly urban sprawl, you just know.

But you might be asking what the business case is for all this beauty, art and emotion. It's a fair question. We need to stay connected with what we care about, otherwise, our work becomes meaningless. How can we care about what we do, our colleagues or our customers if we can't find some emotional connection?

Also, there's a physical case for expression drive having a firm place in our company culture. Music, in particular, has some unique qualities and challenges our brain in a very special way. According to neuroscientist and jazz musician Fred Limb[74] "When we look at the brains of humans, and how they evolved from the brains of animals, it becomes clear rather quickly that the human auditory system is capable of processing sound at an enormous level of complexity, Music, I think, is the highest refinement of that complexity, meaning that as far as I know, there's nothing in the auditory world that is harder for the brain to process than music."

[74.] https://ideas.ted.com/what-making-music-does-to-your-brain/

To process the information in music, especially complex classical music involves different areas of the brain. You literally light up like a Christmas tree when you are listening to Mozart. Spatial-temporal reasoning improves, and it can even reduce stress and lower your blood pressure. Experiments on the so-called "Mozart Effect" have even shown that kids who listen to music might not become more intelligent, but they do get better maths scores![75]

Also, some of the most creative people have the highest Expression drive, and it would be a tragedy if they were missed because they didn't fit some sort of standard business mold.

I think hacking our brains for productivity and enjoyment of what we do is going to be one of the next significant fields of study. Up until now the arts and anything considered 'fluffy' or 'woo-woo' has had a rather poor reception inside organisations but we are going to need to look at this again. Our new generation of workers are not going to stand for doing meaningless or dull work that doesn't involve something that they enjoy. Bringing more things closer to our workplace that appeal to our expression drive can only be a good thing. The challenge will always be how to measure the effects. One thing I do know is that you can certainly measure the effects of people NOT being happy at work; it's VERY expensive.

9.5 The Art In Leadership

Dr Jacquie Drake founded the Praxis Leadership Centre at Cranfield School of Management (UK)[76]. She's a crusader for exceptional leadership and has always taken a very different view about how people make breakthroughs in their ability to manage, lead and influence others. Connection to the arts and taking a different viewpoint has always been

---

[75]. https://www.ncbi.nlm.nih.gov/pmc/articles/PMC1281386
[76]. now a visiting member of faculty there and at Mannheim Business School in Germany.

something that has fascinated her and produced excellent results for many of the senior leaders who she has worked with over the years.

"I love meeting new people." She told me, "When I meet people, I see something in them that's special that they are not aware of. I have an inbuilt desire to help them **express** it, even if they don't know they've got it."

I think we can safely say that Dr Drake is strongly Expression driven (did you notice that she even used the word herself – there are clues everywhere when you are looking for them).

She recalled, "In the early days of Praxis[77] it was the intellectual challenge of how I could help people to do things better (that's discovery drive which we will talk about more later). It was intellectual curiosity backed by a strong desire to see people benefit from what we discovered during our research. Praxis was holistic, in-depth, and innovative. We were always trying new things. I remember looking at how we could use the Shakespeare play Henry V as a case study for leadership, and I wasn't quite sure how to do it. A musician[78] who I invited to Cranfield to do some work on personal presence introduced me to Richard Olivier.[79] Richard had just introduced some people to the leadership themes of the play."

It turned out to be an ideal match at a perfect time. Dr Drake and Olivier worked together for over 6 years. The company that sprang out of that venture, Olivier Mythodrama has grown into a very healthy leadership development business that's still thriving and has an enviable reputation for leadership development using the arts to do it. The lines between emotion, identity, the arts, and leadership are much more blurred than many people first think. Maybe it's time to think again about that.

[77.] At the time a highly experimental leadership faculty inside the Cranfield School of Management.

[78.] There it is again, the expression/artistic connection.

[79.] Son of famous actor Sir Lawrence Olivier.

9.6 Where Art and Business Meet

In many organisations, there doesn't seem to be much talk of the arts. There's a distance between the two worlds. Yet we all connect with stories, and thankfully there is an increasing awareness about story-telling in business. We see stories all the time. They are everywhere and very often we don't think of them as stories. Stories are there as advertisements for products, they are the case studies and testimonials we use to win business. They are the stories told by professional speakers to managers to help people understand important concepts and grasp new ideas. Yet generally, we don't teach people to use stories in the workplace to inspire others. I think we are missing a trick. There are some marvellous storytellers in our organisations, and you can often hear them around the water cooler, but when they get back to their desks, their talents are wasted. I believe we need to make more noise about the power of stories in the workplace and put them to better use.

Also, I think many of us from outside the world of the arts don't always see the level of connection between the two worlds. For example, the British Film, high-end TV, video games, and animation industry[80] is worth a staggering amount of money. In 2015 in the UK alone, the sector attracted over £1.5bn of overseas investment and contributed more than £6bn to the economy. The numbers in the USA, India and other big centres of film production combined are enormous. The arts business is a very big business indeed. Some of the wealthiest and most successful entrepreneurs Britain has ever produced come from the arts sector (for example: Sir Andrew Lloyd-Webber, The Beatles, The Rolling Stones, director Sir Ridley Scott, actors like Anthony Hopkins and writer J K Rowling, and remember that Sir Richard Branson started in the music business with Virgin Records). There are too many others to mention. They make a massive contribution to the economy. What's

---

[80.] http://www.bfi.org.uk/education-research/film-industry-statistics-reports/reports/uk-film-economy/economic-contribution-uks-film-sectors

less well recognised is the contribution that expression, creative thinking and the arts make directly to non-arts driven organisations.

One example of the merging of the two fields is the use of Gamification to engage teams and increase performance and the same principles of games used to take customers on a journey with a company. It's the creativity and imagination of the gamers and the huge economic clout of the gaming industry that has been able to fund the research into the power of a well-designed journey and give us more understanding of the rewards centres in our brains that that light us up.

Around 20 years ago I remember having dinner with a research scientist, Dr Robert E. Horn.[81] Bob developed a writing methodology that increased reader comprehension and performance. His method was commercialised under the brand name Information Mapping® and was based on research on how the human brain works. At that dinner, Bob was in transit on his way back to the USA to work with NASA. He got very excitable when he started telling me about a project he was facilitating there. NASA was using art as a way of coming up with new ideas and solving complex problems using huge murals and infographics. It was a sort of graffiti art that anyone could add to, in fact, people were encouraged to add their random thoughts to the drawing whenever they walked past. It was like a collective string of related views, with each idea and link coming from a different mind. Bob was thrilled to be learning more about how we could deal with 'wicked problems' using the power of pictures. Inside NASA they had started this vast drawing that space engineers would add to as they walked around the circular centre of one of the NASA buildings. Already, the early adoption of his ideas was fuelling cascades of fresh thinking and inspiring one person after another to see things from a different, new perspective. He called his work at the time Visual Design. It was based on new ways of using

---

[81.] **Robert E. Horn** information scientist who taught at Harvard, Columbia, and Sheffield (U.K) and has been a visiting scholar at Stanford University's Center for the Study of Language and Information. He is known for the development of Information Mapping®.

art and our natural way of thinking in pictures (which many of us do before we think of using language). The use of infographics, which are so popular today come from research like that where business, projects, and art collides.

When you think about how much business information is stored and communicated in words it makes sense to consider that if we need to solve the really complex problems that humanity is facing, we need another method. The use of art, drawing and visuals make perfect sense.

Today we are all living in a media based world. All the anecdotal evidence points more and more towards a world where telling human stories is the way to get our message across. With the advent of social media, movie quality video cameras inside our pockets at all times we are all becoming stars, directors and scriptwriters. Surely, it's time we picked up on that and brought it into our workplaces and started using more video.

Expression drive is becoming more fashionable too. I'll hazard a guess that it is related to the fact that social media is allowing all of us to express what we feel and communicate our passions and pet hates to others. Young people, in particular, care more and more about what business does and what it stands for.

Our future workforce is getting ever more concerned with working at organisations with a conscience. They aren't attracted just by money. The young people starting today in our workforce, and the generations coming in over the next decade are going to be the most purpose and conscience-driven generation that we have ever seen. Only the other day I was talking to Paul Hargreaves, the CEO of a large food distribution firm who told me that all his new staff were millennials. They were attracted by the values of the business and the idea of using business to do good. The CEO had a vision from the beginning that his company was going to do something socially useful, and his support for an orphanage in Africa has been just one of the ways he is making his business purposeful. His company is becoming more and more about its contribution as well as its ability to make a profit for profit's sake[82]. "After all, he said, "business from the Victorian age onwards has done massive damage to people, culture and the environment and it's up to us to start using business to put things right." I couldn't agree more.

9.7 Expression Drive is Connected To Our Identity

What we do for a living is tightly bound to our identity, so it's hardly surprising that some clever companies have taken this idea to the limit. In his book 'Payoff', Dan Ariely talks about his personal experiences with Ikea furniture and their diabolical, hard to understand instructions and missing parts. When he eventually worked out what he needed to do to put the damn thing together he experienced a strange sense of satisfaction, "I stood back looking at the chest and smiled with pride at having completed the job. Over the years, I've noticed that I look at that chest of drawers more often, and more fondly, than any other piece of furniture in my house." He and his colleagues labelled that feeling as "The Ikea Effect". He goes on to talk about the failure of cake mixes that make it too easy for us (we don't feel like we have really made the cake) so food manufacturers took out the egg powder and made us work a bit harder. The cake mixes then flew off the shelves. What Ariely is explaining is that what we get pleasure from is directly linked to our own efforts and what we create becomes part of our identity. What we do really does have an effect on who we are.

Nowhere is our expression and our identity better expressed than in our homes. We surround ourselves with things we love and decorate with colours that soothe or stimulate us. I remember reading John

---

[82.] MD of Cotswold Fayre Ltd, Paul Hargreaves, author of forthcoming book *Accidentally on Purpose*. His company is also a B-Corporation. See www.bcorporation.net for details of this purpose driven business movement.

Demartini's book *Inspired Destiny* where he suggests that if you are looking for a new direction and aren't yet clear what it is then just look round your home. The clues are all there. Look at what's clean and well looked after versus what is thrown in the back of your cupboards. I looked around my house and saw that books had pride of place and the things that made my animals comfortable next, with everything else fitting in around them.

Expression drive helps us to connect with our identity. Of all the motivations it's the one that most closely connects us to the essence of who we really are. That's why, despite it's hard to pin down nature, we need to welcome it into our organisations and companies and not be scared of it.

9.8 Learning Summary

So, what have we learned about Expression Motivation?

- Expression motivated people need to connect
- They are often highly artistic
- Their talents are often overlooked in a business context – big mistake!
- They are great at connecting random ideas
- They often have a great sense of timing
- Emotional intelligence is a strong trait
- Allow them to express themselves
- They care – passionately – about a lot of things

Key Words: Trust. Beauty. Humanity

9.9 Black Belt Expression Strategies

Black Belt Leaders ...

- Encourage people to express themselves
- Give people the confidence to speak up
- Coach people to channel their emotions effectively instead of destructively
- Don't judge emotions, they accept them and process them
- Encourage creativity
- Don't accept formalised processes as the only way to do things
- Are always looking for beautiful solutions
- Encourage people's creative pursuits outside work
- Read books that expand their own horizons
- See the beauty in things
- Recognise great work

Chapter 10

Discovery Motivation

10.1 Curiosity Didn't Kill The Cat

We are inquisitive creatures. We spend vast amounts of time doing utterly unproductive things, learning about things we don't have any use for or exploring places that we won't ever visit again. We are driven to discover things, or as the late American author, Kurt Vonnegut said, "We are here on Earth to fart around. Don't let anybody tell you any different."

We love to know the answers to lots of things even if there's no apparent benefit to us. For some of us, it's a way of passing the time or keeping variety in our lives but for others, curiosity and the drive to discover new things is a way of life. It's what gets some people up in the morning.

The Discovery flame is behind many of the great innovations of our time. It's the curiosity that fuels the big questions. Give a challenge to a Discovery driven person and instead of immediately going off and trying to fix things (which is what a Results driven person would likely do), instead you will be barraged by questions. They will want to know the nature of the problem so that they can get to the most interesting angles to explore.

Man's curiosity is what took us to the moon, will take us to Mars, discovered the healing power of penicillin and is the intellectual horse-power behind the great philosophers who've profoundly affected our laws, our morals and how we treat each other. If you want to get the right answers to useful questions, you need to be curious enough to want to know what's going on. Professor Steven Hawking passed away while I was writing the final draft of this section about Discovery drive and it was a sight to see thousands of people lining the streets of Cambridge where he lived and worked on the day of his funeral. His book, *A Brief History of Time* captivated people even if they didn't understand much of it. Hawking's own passion for asking questions that mattered and searching for solutions about the big ideas of our day captured the hearts and minds of people all over the world.

Famous Discovery driven people include Sir David Attenborough, whose curiosity about nature and animals have captivated TV audiences for over 50 years, and Professor Brian Cox, the rock and roll playing academic physicist who has such a passion for his subject you can almost feel his energy moving from the TV screen and into the living room when he is on TV. These people are great examples of Discovery drive in action.

Think back to the NASA story and to Dr Robert Horn's massive infographic; art might have been the medium to solve the big challenges, but the people walking around the halls of the NASA building were all there because they were curious – not because they were artistic.

10.2 Discovery Motivation Summary Table

DISCOVERY MOTIVATION

INDICATORS

Questioning. Interested. Naturally curious. Creative. Dynamic thinker. Eclectic mix of interests. Purpose driven. Makes unexpected connections because of their wide range of interests. Ability to hold multiple viewpoints to generate new perspectives. Great at cross-fertilising ideas. Easily bored. Needs variety. Highly innovative. Challenges convention. Ideas factory. Inspires others. Dynamic and visionary style of leadership. Vivid imagination.

FIRED UP BY

New things. Bold ideas. 'Wicked" problems. Variety. Lifelong learning. Novel ideas. Unusual challenges. Intellectual rigour. Debates with the interesting people. Books. Staying up to date with technology and science. Wants to know about new developments. Intellectual horsepower.

FLAME EXTINGUISHED BY

Boredom. Monotony. Lack of intellectual stimulation. No room for experimentation. Poor quality content that isn't thought through properly. Lack of information. Poor research. Small talk. Inflexible thinking of others. Anything (or anyone) with lack of depth or intellectual substance. Zero risk taking.

Keywords – Interesting. Intellectually challenging.

10.3 The Mysteries of the Universe

Christian Kromme is a futurologist and one of the most curious people I know. His background is in technology, and he's fascinated with how everything works and fits together. What gets Christian fired up are the really big questions like 'how do nature and technology work together?' and 'how is the universe like the human brain?' His fascination and curiosity are infectious. After selling his technology company, he has made a new career from his curiosity and is an in-demand futurist speaking on the international conference circuit. He has rapidly built a strong reputation for his unfettered imagination and his foresight. Many of the predictions he made a few years ago when I first met him have already come true.

Christian's daughter was born with a rare genetic condition. The doctors didn't give her long to live, no more than a few months if they were lucky. But Christian has a powerful discovery drive and he started to ask questions that no one had asked before. He researched everything he could get his hands on that didn't appear related to her condition; how cells respond to light, how they communicate and what was going on at the cutting edge of DNA research. There is no doubt that it was Christian's discovery drive that saved his daughters' life. Lieke is now at school, going to play with her friends and is leading a full life.

When I asked him, what motivated him the answer was immediate, "I'm fascinated by everything; how consciousness works, how the world works and how everything fits together. The universe is an amazing place, I believe it's all connected from the tiniest particle to the biggest organism, I can't imagine that I will ever run out of things to explore."

10.3. Making Big Discoveries

Being driven by the Discovery flame is not something reserved only for those with a university education. The most curious people around are kids under 5. They are continually exploring and asking questions.

When kids' curiosity and creativity is encouraged and supported, they are more likely to grow into curious adults, but not everyone has a supportive start in life.

David Thomson didn't have much space for curiosity when he was a kid. He was too busy surviving. His stepfather was a violent man who hit his mum. David and his sister were regularly locked in the bedroom while the grown-ups went out drinking. He told me he wanted to be rich and tough because as a child, the family had no money and no food. The family was repeatedly evicted, and as a little boy, he used to have to steal food by digging up potatoes from the local allotments under cover of darkness. He ended up bouncing around different children's homes and relatives and went to six different schools by the time he was 11 years old. You get the theme here. This is not someone who came from a background where traditional education and books were valued. The only thing that mattered to his parents was going to the pub on a Saturday night and having enough money to gamble away at the bookies. It left David and his little sister facing a choice; do you let this define you, or make a different choice?

I'll let David pick up the story himself, "My life had always been disorganised and violent, my schooling erratic and my knowledge would have fitted on the back of a postage stamp and still enough room left to write the Lord's Prayer. I'd won titles at boxing and athletics, served four years in the British Army and come out after a cheeky ploy with two scars and £6,000 in compensation – enough to pay off my debts and buy a green Ford Capri my mates called 'Kermit.' I had returned to Kettering, where I grew up, and secured a job as head of packing and dispatch at R. Griggs Airwair boot factory, where they made the famous bovver boots."

It was 1991 and David had just turned 21. He was packing another pair of Doc Martens boots when he realised that if he didn't do something now, he was going to be packing boots for the rest of his life. Then, out of the blue, he got his first taste of what it was like to voyage into the world of discovery when he was given an unexpected gift of a book. It was unexpected because David is dyslexic, "I had only read the Peter and Jane Ladybird books[83] and, at nine, that was about it. The brother-in-law of my girlfriend gave me *The Success System That Never Fails*, by William Clement Stone. I now held in my hands this odd gift, a book that I probably wouldn't have read had it not been for the title. I sat down between the boxes in the shoe factory, started reading and the words seemed to jump off the page at me. William Clement Stone talked about success in terms of having a positive mental attitude, that in any given set of circumstances you must incorporate the plus traits of life."

David's journey had started, and he wouldn't look back. He's a great example that a little knowledge and a lot of action goes a long way. David took action and got a job with Clement Stone's company that sent him on a two-week course at the Station Hotel in Derby, the course concentrated on Positive Mental Attitude. He lapped up the knowledge and was fascinated by the topics, psychology, inertia, systems and processes, and even the philosophy of Socrates. But despite the crash course and his determination (that included studying until 3am every night during the course) he struggled to make ends meet on the commission-only pay packet, and he ended up back at the shoe factory. It was just a setback. He told me over 20 years later that he reacts differently to setbacks, "Most people go inert when there is a problem or a challenge. When you go inert, that's the closest thing to having a negative mental attitude. Most people don't go negative. What they tend to do is they just sit around and do nothing. How can you ever achieve anything unless you are taking action? You gotta take action! It's amazing where you end up. It's about having that dedication."

He didn't stay packing boots for long. His next job was as a mortgage consultant. He saw a job advert asking "<u>Are you positive and enthusiastic? Do you go the extra mile? Are you the kind of person who is</u>

[83.] A famous series of books to develop early stage reading skills created by a teacher, William Murray, who became headmaster of a school for school for the educationally subnormal" in Cheltenham, England.

persuasive?" Yes, I said to myself. They'll call me. I didn't even know how to spell mortgage, but I applied anyway. After six interviews I got the job and had a feeling when I walked out of the shoe factory at the end of the week that this time it was going to be the last time. As I set off that first morning for my new job, I reached into the glove box and grabbed three cassette tapes. They were 'Back to Life Back to Reality', by Soul to Soul, a reminder of my army days, and a personal development tape I had picked up after reading *The Success System That Never Fails*. It occurred to me that I would be spending ten minutes in the car each day going to work and ten minutes driving home, that's twenty minutes a day; 100 minutes a week, 400 minutes a month, 4,000 minutes in a working year; if I worked ten months a year, I could either learn something new or just piss about listening to the radio like everyone else, I chose to learn. It was one of the best things I've ever done."

There's David's other flame right there. Results. You can see that how he measures things and sets clear goals is one of the things that sets him apart. Interestingly, I first met him at an event where the keynote speaker was my friend Brian Tracy, author of *Eat That Frog* who you met earlier in this book. Brian's work is focused on goal setting and becoming successful, and he was one of the speakers on those early tapes that David listened to in his car. That decision to listen to his first personal development tapes he credits as being one of the key things that changed his life. "There was something else that helped me," he recalled. "I had always been poor. To me, a penny was a penny, a pound was a pound, and a fiver was a lot of money. Other brokers may have said, oh, don't worry, it's only an extra few quid a month. But I was able to see it from the clients' perspective. Working people applying for a mortgage, often for the first time, have a lot to think about and an extra few quid is money always better off in their pockets than somebody else's."

Then he went on to tell me about something really important that I believe we can all learn from, David calls them Golden Moments, "At lunchtime that first day I went to McDonald's in my company tie. I felt in the bright surroundings that I had arrived, that my life was beginning that moment. I still remember to this day." Where did that appreciation come from, I asked him, "As a kid, I learned how to survive and how to make the most of any small perk or moment of joy. There was often no food in the house, there were occasions when I was six years old, and it was way past my bedtime when Jimmy (David's stepfather) would take me out to the allotments and we'd dig with our bare hands looking for potatoes. We'd take them home, mum would make a big pan of chips and no chips have ever tasted so delicious."

His appreciation for those golden moments was rooted in poverty not in wealth. Many years later, David is celebrating a different sort of success; he has just sold his own financial services firm for a seven-figure sum. "Because I'd had a poor education, I had to learn things like a five-year-old and then, I was able to explain the financial packages in a way that even a five-year-old would understand. Some brokers skimmed over details or didn't clarify the small print. I plodded my way through slowly and the clients were grateful when they 'got it.'"

It proves that there is more than one type of discovery. It's not all about scientific breakthroughs or discovering the far-flung reaches of the universe. Sometimes the most fascinating things to learn about is what's really going on between your own ears.

Another entrepreneur, Dan Miller from Derby (who was just 20 years old at the time of writing), is yet another dyslexic person with a fascination for discovering how things work. He sees the world in a different way to most people, "When I see something I like I want to know how it's made, how much does it sell for, what the margins are. When I worked in a pub behind a bar I wanted to know what the margins were on the cocktails."

Dan is dyslexic, and he struggled with traditional study, yet at 17 years old he created an events business from his bedroom and put 700 students, sponsors, and prospective employers in an event venue together. His first paying clients were PWC and his second was Rolls Royce. He moved to London because things weren't moving fast enough for his business.[84] Within two weeks of being there he had raised £50,000 in capital to fund the development of an app for students where they could search for apprenticeships and graduate job opportunities on their phone. He is incredibly curious and from the moment you sit down with him, he never stops asking questions. His childlike curiosity is his biggest strength.

There are plenty of famous dyslexic success stories and Sir Richard Branson, founder of the Virgin Group, is one of the most famous of all. Although it is still the case that dyslexia can cause problems at school, Branson and many others prove that it's only a disability if you think it is. The same goes for ADHD (Attention Deficit Hyperactive Disorder, sometimes referred to as Attention Deficit Disorder or ADD). A high proportion of people with dyslexia have ADD too. One of the most respected marketers and founder of the global business Strategic Coach®, Dan Sullivan has ADHD. Sullivan collaborated with one of the worlds' leading authorities on the minds of entrepreneurs, Dr Edward (Ned) Hallowell, a Harvard Medical School faculty member and a licensed psychologist who in a recent interview said: "I think we should rename ADD as the entrepreneurial trait."

Sullivan had worked with thousands of entrepreneurs, Hallowell had worked with ADD patients and they realised that they had been working with many of the same people!

10.4 Dinosaurs, Darwin and Discovery

Many of the outstanding discoveries of our age have been made by discovery-driven academics who have travelled through the formal education system. Learning something new for its own sake gives people with high Discovery drive a huge buzz. For them, the **process** of discovery can be more important than the discovery itself.

[84.] Dan is CEO of Young Professionals UK www.young-professionals.uk

Professor Norman MacLeod BSc, MSc, PhD, FGS, FLS (you have to do a hell of a lot of research to get that many letters after your name) is a senior research scientist at The Natural History Museum in London. He's also Honorary Professor at University College London and Visiting Professor at the Nanjing Institute of Geology and Palaeontology, Chinese Academy of Sciences. As you can see, he's a seriously clever dude. MacLeod is one of life's curious people. He has been working on Artificial Intelligence for many years, long before A.I hit the headlines, but he didn't start out with the intention of becoming a leading academic working at the cutting edge of science, but he has always loved puzzles and has had a fascination with animals and nature.

He didn't start out as a gifted student. He didn't fly through school and he wasn't an early high flyer inside the academic ranks. Initially, his academic focus came from the desire not to be shown up by the master's degree students who were younger than him. "That's when I started buckling down to my studies."

The professor always had a passion and a fascination for animals. In the summer of 2017, he was walking through a little French village with some friends when he heard a cicada, the noisy little critters had been the topic of conversation over dinner the night before. "It seemed to me that it was in one of the trees, so I hopped over the wall. I wanted to show it to my friends as they had never seen one close up before. I still get the feeling of what I can only describe as joy that comes over me when I see this little piece of life staring back at me. Even when I was a little kid, I've always had that. I remember when my mom used to squash bugs in the house it used to make me physically sick."

"For me, science feels like a desire to explore," he told me. He's curious about lots of things, not just his specialist fields (he has more than one!). "I like to travel between different fields of expertise. A colleague once told me that whenever he had a new idea and entered a new field that he thinks no-one else has worked on before and started reading the literature, he got sight of my coat-tails as I was already disappearing around the next corner!"

It's been a while since we talked about Inclusion motivation. The professor is a great example of someone who has low levels of it; he's not big on small talk. He was comfortable to tell me that he has a decidedly low tolerance for such things, a low tolerance for being bored and was happy to label himself as, at times, anti-social. "I'd rather be exploring something interesting." His discovery undoubtedly drives his life and work and he has a level of results drive too, "I'm a consistent worker and I'm practical and results oriented. I'm a good starter of projects and a good completer of projects".

Curious minds are everywhere. In our universities and research centres, in our kindergartens and in our businesses. So, stay curious and encourage other people to remain curious too. It's the spice of life.

That raises a very useful connection between curiosity and its link to success.

10.5 Neo and The Matrix

The social scientist Dr Carol Dweck, Professor of Psychology at Stanford University wrote a book called *Mindset*.[85] In the book, she makes a precise definition between people who have a fixed mindset and those who have a growth mindset. She observed that people with a fixed mindset seek approval; those with a growth mindset seek development and guess what flame fuels a growth mindset? Yes, it's discovery. It's curiosity that is the hallmark of having, or developing, a growth mindset.

In the film The Matrix, Neo (played by Keanu Reeves) is offered the choice between two pills by Morpheus (Laurence Fishburne), "This is your last chance. After this, there is no turning back. You take the blue pill—the story ends, you wake up in your bed and believe whatever you want to believe [Fixed Mindset] You take the red pill—you stay in

---

[85.] *Mindset: The New Psychology of Success*, recently updated and published by Robinson 2017.

Wonderland, and I show you how deep the rabbit hole goes [Growth Mindset]. Remember: all I'm offering is the truth. Nothing more." The red pill is the one that will allow Neo to follow his curiosity. The blue pill keeps him in ignorance locked in his grey world with no chance of progress. Morpheus tells Neo "You have been born into a prison for your mind", in a way, that's exactly what a fixed mindset does.

Dweck's important work covers many aspects of our attitude to learning, failure, resilience and grasping opportunities. She also makes a key distinction with how we react to failure and it turns out that our attitude towards learning new things and our innate curiosity is one of the things that helps to reframe how we see failure.

By looking at the things that go wrong at work and in life as lessons, we are able to learn from our mistakes, we have the tools to turn adversity into a valuable learning experience. It's all about re-framing our experience and not just about having a different experience.

Study after study tells us that discovering something new is good for us. It keeps life interesting, helps us to keep our brain function in tip-top condition and positively affects your mood. It's damn useful at dinner parties too … Just don't end up being a smartass. No one likes people who think they know everything, but people do connect with people who *want* to know everything. That's infectious, fascinating and fun.

10.6 The Quiz Loving Nun's Secret

It turns out that Discovery drive isn't just something that helps you succeed and be happier, it's good for you too. Sister Bernadette was a nun who lived in Mankato, Minnesota in the USA. She had been taking part in a long-term study by a scientist called David Snowdon.[86] She was one of the School Sisters of Notre Dame, an order of nuns who

---

[86.] Study highlighted inside a book called *Spark: How exercise will improve the performance of your brain* by Dr John J Ratey and Eric Hagerman published by Quercus.

took part in a long-term study on brain health. The nuns thrived on stretching their minds and discovering new things. Each day they tackled quizzes, puzzles, and stretched their vocabulary and engaged in thought-provoking debates. Sister Bernadette also kept teaching late into life and scored highly (being in the 90th percentile in the cognitive tests set by the research team) right up until the age of 85, when she sadly died of a heart attack.

Sister Bernadette donated her brain to science after her death, as did more than six hundred other nuns. When the researchers studied her brain they made a startling discovery; it was ravaged by massive damage from Alzheimer's disease. She had even carried a particular gene variant that indicated she was genetically predisposed to it and by most conventional measures she would have been expected to barely be able to function unassisted to survive day to day, yet she demonstrated no visible signs of dementia during her lifetime. The researchers believe that she remained mentally sharp because of the way she lived, despite the damage. She had a strong social circle and support network (inclusion) and challenged her brain every day.

The lesson that teaches us all is that curiosity and connection are more than just fun. It can play a vital role in a long and healthy life too.

10.7 Discoveries Win Prizes – but it's not why we do it

Elizabeth Blackburn is a biologist who shared the Nobel Prize for Medicine in 2009. She discovered how the ends of chromosomes are protected by structures called telomeres (telomeres protective ends on your DNA that work like the little end caps of shoelaces and they protect your DNA from 'fraying' and degenerating). That process is called ageing, to you and me. Blackburn had started her career as a biologist studying a single-celled animal that lives on the water, fondly known as pond scum. She was fascinated by one strange characteristic that sets it apart from most other animals. It doesn't age. Pond scum DNA never deteriorates.

Blackburn has always been curious and is definitely Discovery driven. She relates in her TED[87] talk, "It was no surprise I became a scientist. Growing up far away from here, as a little girl I was deadly curious about everything alive. I used to pick up lethally poisonous stinging jellyfish and sing to them. And so, starting my career, I was deadly curious about fundamental mysteries of the most basic building blocks of life, and I was fortunate to live in a society where that curiosity was valued".

Blackburn and her teams' research prompted many other studies into ageing. In her 2017 TED talk, she shared the fact that there have now been over 10,000 peer-reviewed studies that prove conclusively that our levels of stress and how we respond to it directly impacts our DNA repair mechanisms. In other words, how we react under stress has been proven to directly dictate how quickly our cells age. When DNA no longer repairs itself our skin wrinkles, our hair goes grey, and a whole host of other processes inside our bodies become more susceptible to disease and breakdown.

In one fascinating study done at UCLA, Blackburn shared how the researchers had discovered that mothers who were long-term caregivers to children with complex needs like learning difficulties, severe autism or physical limitations (anything that put mothers under prolonged and higher than normal levels of maternal stress) had shorter DNA strands. They also had more damage to the ends of their DNA than people who didn't live with such levels of long-term stress. But what was really fascinating was that the researchers were able to prove that just 12 minutes of meditation a day was able to re-establish the protective telomeres that would slow down the ageing process of their cells.

If ever there was a scientific argument for stress reduction in the workplace and meditation to improve your quality of life, there it is. The point here is that Elizabeth Blackburn's discovery drive has the

---

87. https://www.ted.com/talks/elizabeth_blackburn_the_science_of_cells_that_never _get_old

direct power to affect your life right now. Now you know that the effects of ageing are something that you can choose to do something about, you have the power to protect your own DNA. People who ask great questions, intriguing questions and strange questions so often find themselves as the change makers. Encourage curiosity and discovery in your world. Ask great questions and foster the idea that there are very few, if any, silly questions. The most off the wall ideas often lead to practical solutions to everyday problems. It's people who have an intense curiosity about the world who make momentous breakthroughs. Just imagine if Elizabeth Blackburn had been told to stop wasting her time asking questions about pond scum by someone who couldn't see the relevance of it. Just think what the world would have missed! Who knows where that research will take us in the next few decades, and all because of her enquiring mind. Her discovery drive has the potential to help us all live longer and healthier lives. Discovery motivation is what fuels innovation, progress and the big shifts that change our world.

10.8 How Flames Work Together

One of the fascinating things for me is when there are strong combinations of the different flames. Ioan Smith, Economist and founder of Semaphore Macro, has a mix of discovery drive, flow drive, and results drive. They run like a golden thread through both work life and leisure time.

Discovery is the hot flame for Ioan. He has an inquisitive mind. In his business, he pores over a staggering amount of macroeconomic data and turns out a remarkable stream of coherent, connected commentary and daily snapshots of world economic data. I know: I get the data. Every day. Reams of it. I don't know how he does it. Just as I was writing this piece, a captivating email just arrived from Ioan informing me of the dip in investor confidence in Germany and a spike 10-year bond yield of .736% – Riveting stuff. It was the 8th message so far this morning.

You get the idea, the quantity and quality of data this guy can scan, interpret and digest into a manageable format for his clients is staggering. He's regularly quoted by sources like CNBC and other financial media. As it happens, he also happens to be very funny, and some of the headlines on his emails have me laughing out loud. Ioan had the world's most unlikely start as an economist. It's an inspiring story that demonstrates that if you are fascinated enough by something and have a determination to succeed, then there's very little that can get in your way over the long term. So how does a kid from a poverty-stricken part of South Wales end up as a leading economic thinker who has the power to sell his ideas and information to global banks, hedge funds and investors?

Well, first thing is that you have to be curious. Wildly curious. Even as a kid, Ioan was fascinated with penny shares. His monthly penny stock newsletter dropping onto his doormat was the highlight of his month. His capacity for taking in information was evident right at the start, a little strange for a kid living deep in the proud but poor Valley's area of South Wales. Life was tough. His mother worked in dull jobs in local factories and he was determined that there was a better way to live. After gaining a degree, he spent a period working in the Small Firms Research unit at Cardiff University and as a result had a chance meeting with Chief Economist at Lehman Brothers, John Llewellyn who offered him a job there. At the time Lehman Bros was a behemoth of a firm and Llewellyn went on to become Economic Advisor to Her Majesty's Treasury.

He spent two years doing grunt work; then he finally found a sideways route onto the graduate program and eventually edged his way into trading. A few more moves and he was MD of the research division at a large hedge fund. He found his niche, and created the role for himself that he loved to do; independent research. Ioan was quick to point out that he gets into a flow state when he is doing his research. What often starts out as a drive to learn, discover new things and make new connections between ideas and information turns into flow. "To get into a flow state of mind, you really have to be interested in something. A lot of the time it's not the end goal but it's the process itself that's enjoyable" he told me. In his free time, his flow drive also appears. He talks about the high that athletes describe, that hit of dopamine. That rush that your body gives you when you go past the initial pain of the warm-up – only in his time off he gets into flow with other people. "When I climbed Kilimanjaro, I was overcome by emotion. When I finish a marathon or do a 5km swim, the camaraderie is such a big part of it. Those experiences in life where you try to further yourself, prove to yourself that you can do things, overcoming adversity and pushing yourself to the limit. I've always wanted to be inspired – and inspire as well."

Isn't that what we all want?

10.9 Follow Your Curiosity

But following your passion is one of the worst ideas to help you get ahead, according to billionaire Mark Cuban. In an interview for the Amazon Insights for Entrepreneurs Series (feel free to tweet the Amazon team & put this book forward for that – I'd be up for it, Mr Bezos …), Cuban said "One of the great lies of life is 'follow your passion'. Everybody tells you, 'follow your passion, follow your passion.'"

Cuban says that's bad advice because you may not excel at what you are passionate about, "I used to be passionate to be a baseball player. Then I realised I had a 70-mile-per-hour fastball," says Cuban. "Competitive major league pitchers throw fastballs 20 miles per hour faster than that." Despite all his enthusiasm he just didn't have the natural talent. One of Cuban's strengths was to recognise that and then to spend his time doing something more useful and productive instead. "There are a lot of things I am passionate about. A lot," says Cuban. Instead, he advises you to pay attention to those things that you devote time to.

"The things I ended up being really good at were the things I found myself putting effort into. A lot of people talk about passion, but that's really not what you need to focus on. You really need to evaluate and say, 'Okay, where am I putting in my time? Because when you look at where you put in your time, where you put in your effort that tends to be the things that you are good at. And if you put in enough time, you tend to get really good at it. Nobody quits anything they are good at because it is fun to be good. It is fun to be one of the best, but to be one of the best, you must put in effort. So, don't follow your passions, follow your effort," says Cuban.

Jeff Chaplin agrees. Chaplin is a co-founder of revolutionary Internet mattress company Caspar.[88] Chaplin calls passion 'whimsical', "There are so many things that can captivate you that don't have to do with your passions," he told CNBC. Often hearing the advice "follow your passion" translates into following your hobby. "I love kitesurfing, so I'm going to go start a kitesurfing business," Chapin says, as an example. "The reality is, you probably ruined your hobby because now you turned your passion into your job."

Chaplin has a point. That exact thing happened to me when I recently took my ski instructor exams. I realised that my passion for skiing would quickly slide away if I spent enough Sunday afternoon's picking other people's screaming toddlers up off a soggy ski slope. So, I decided to stick to the day job, and hope I can do it well enough to keep paying for the ski holidays.

Vets, Coaches and Other Curious People

Max Tuck is a qualified and practising vet. Veterinary medicine is a notoriously difficult course, and it has a reputation for being one of the most punishing academic courses there is. Once qualified, it's also a career that's not for the faint-hearted. Long days, late night calls and a job full of highlights and heart-wrenching moments. If you're not highly motivated, you are not likely to last very long as a vet. As well as qualifying to

---

[88.] sourced from article from the CNBC Make It series.

be a vet in the first place (despite at least one person in her life telling her she wasn't bright enough), Max has a few extra things up her sleeve for her evenings, weekends, and holidays. She is a published author of several books about nutrition and optimum health in humans. She's a world-renowned expert on raw and living foods, a marathon runner, a triathlete and a black belt in karate. She runs raw food retreats and all sorts of diet and lifestyle courses in her 'spare' time and is fanatical about achieving peak performance and helping others reach it too. Max's achievements before breakfast leave most people breathless. She speaks quickly (so much to share; too little time). When I asked Max about her books, and she was quick to tell me that she had been declined by 11 publishers before she found someone that was prepared to give her first book a chance. Quite simply, she wasn't prepared to give up. It's the on-going possibilities of new discoveries and making lives better that keeps Max fired up. She's always researching something. Her discovery drive makes her a fascinating (and very knowledgeable) person to listen to. She found her flame and now her motivation takes care of itself.

Tony Selimi arrived in England from the war-ravaged Balkan region and found himself homeless on the streets of London not knowing if he would ever see his family again. To stay curious when your life is at that level of challenge demonstrates one heck of a level of discovery drive, "people looked at me as if I was an animal. It was fascinating for me to observe that." he commented. A few years later he had turned his chaotic early life around. He has turned his curiosity into a career. Tony has spoken at conferences and events all over the world and has written two books to date and has a thriving coaching practice, "When you open up a conversation with another human being from a place of curiosity, you can open doors and rooms in their head that they consistently conceal. We are so good at upgrading our technology, but we aren't so good at upgrading ourselves. When I was homeless, people walked past me as if I were a stray dog. "We are so quick to judge what we don't understand" he told me. He now makes a living from asking people great questions.

The future belongs to the curious because all the mundane and thoughtless jobs and outputs will be the remit of the robots. There's no stopping progress. Robots are more predictable than we are. They are cheaper than we are, and they don't complain, go off sick with the flu or ask for a pay rise. The future belongs to the new explorers. The future belongs to the Discovery-driven. The innovations that are going to change how we live, how we power and preserve our planet and how we feed ourselves is going to come from the innovators who will ask the right questions and have the flame of their discovery drive propelling them (and us) forward.

10.10 What Helps Discovery Driven People To Be More Successful

It goes without saying that if you can't communicate all the amazing things you discover, then you aren't going to do much good with what you find out! Communication skills are essential for discovery-driven people if their ideas are going to come to life. Think about scientists such as TV cosmologist and physicist Professor Brian Cox. When he appears on TV talking about anything, his enthusiasm for his discoveries pour out of the screen. You can almost feel him in the room with you. He's become really good at using metaphors to explain complex concepts and it has endeared him to the nation. I remember being captivated by his explanation of how gravity affects the formation of snowflakes. He wove all sorts of advanced concepts into the narrative. He's a genius communicator. Sir David Attenborough shares those same communication skills. When you trust yourself to communicate your ideas you become more confident. When other people trust you, you become credible.

10.11 Learning Summary

So, what have we learned about Discovery Motivated People?

- Curiosity is the fuel behind all innovation
- Their discovery mindset challenges convention
- They love asking questions – sometimes awkward ones!
- Are easily bored and need interesting things to do
- Have contagious positive energy
- They love puzzles and conundrums
- They are great problem solvers
- Can become visionary leaders
- Ask great questions
- Never Run out of ideas

Discovery Drive Black Belt Strategies

Black Belt Leaders . . .

- Keep stretching and challenging people
- Provide variety
- Provide a stabilising influence to counteract randomness
- Manage team and organisational focus well
- Listen to off the wall ideas before the judge them
- Know when the research must stop, and action must begin
- Allow people to experiment within well-considered boundaries
- Encourage innovation and curiosity

Key Words – Innovation. Variety. Fascination.

Chapter 11

Applying the 5 Flames to your Life and Work

11.1 The Flames In Action

There are lots of ways to use the 5 flames. Here are a few ideas to get you started.

One of my executive coaching clients owns and runs a factory producing home fragrance products. The Founder and MD, Doug Wren, saw the Flames Card[89] and put it to use straight away with his team. He scrolls through the flames throughout the day to keep things fresh and help the team and here's how he does it. The team starts the day making sure everything on the production line is fully prepared and ready to go, all the equipment they need is close to hand. All the packaging they are going to use is accessible and all the workstations are prepared. This gives the team the best possible chance to get into **flow**. The last thing they want is to be interrupted and lose focus when they are on a roll.

During the breaks, the supervisors make sure that everyone is being included in the rest areas and no one is being shunned or left out. The **inclusion** flame has helped them become more aware of the group dynamic and the requirement to show leadership. Then they have '**Results** *power-hours*' where they set competitions and play games to see

---

[89.] Go to my website to download your free copy and print it for your desk or your team to use. www.sophiebennett.com/resources

who can produce the most products inside a clearly defined quality standard in, say, 30 minutes.

For expression, they make sure they are giving everyone a voice during the working day (they use coffee breaks and walks around the factory floor during the day with a deliberate focus on making sure everyone is listened to) so that people feel they are listened to by the bosses – and each other. If people aren't happy, they get to find out early enough to do something about it. They pick up on problems and get to nip them in the bud.

Finally, they use the discovery flame to keep improving the work environment, the production process and how they do things. They do it by encouraging questions from the team and staying open-minded. They even initiated a 'Discovery 5' at the end of each shift. They spend just five minutes taking suggestions on what they could do better or more efficiently for the business, or what they could do to make work more fun for the team.

They have found a way to encourage a growth mindset by using the flames. I would never have thought of scrolling through them like that! That's the great thing about letting your ideas out into the world and standing up themselves; people do really creative stuff with them.

Use the Flames to Develop Courageous Leadership

The flames are also a great management and leadership training tool. A quick glance at the postcard can help people to stay on track during day-to-day life and work. They help people to remain aware of the things that matter:

- **Flow** – Helps people to move towards mastery and getting focused. It helps people find a working rhythm and teams to find their flow. Micromanagement isn't possible when the focus is creating and facilitating flow at work.

- **I**nclusion – By focusing on including people, listening to them and bringing the best out in them, you build emotional intelligence. You can spot negative behaviours between people early enough to prevent a toxic atmosphere taking hold. You make unexpected connections with people and deepen relationships.
- **R**esults – Getting results and making sure there are clear goals and milestones is good for everyone. Being clear about what's expected helps people to live up to expectations and know when they have succeeded. Rewarding results with recognition allows people to enjoy a sense of personal achievement and satisfaction for a job well done.
- **E**xpression – By making sure we stay connected to our emotions, we stay connected to who we really are. By developing the courage to say what we mean and communicate openly we build stronger more trusting relationships and become more respected and relied upon by others. We can only keep our word when we are honest with ourselves.
- **D**iscovery – By staying playful, we stay innovative. Never stop asking great questions and staying curious. It's the lifeblood of new ideas and is the source of exciting diversions that keep life fun.

Using the Flames Outside Work to Build a Better Life
On a personal level, you can use the flames too. Here are some ideas that you might find useful:

For Flow – keep finding ways to improve your focus. You will achieve more, get in flow more often and have a much greater level of satisfaction from your daily life. Become a champion of flow and a source of great flow energy. Give yourself time to meditate if that's your thing, it's a proven way to reduce stress and access your creative side.

For Inclusion – Look for new ways to include people in the things that you do. Your life and work will improve when you feel more connected to people. The world's longest-running study of what contributes to a happy, healthy life, (run by Harvard[90] University)[91] is unequivocal; our relationships have more impact on how long we live, how happy we are and our brain health than any other indicator. So, join a mentoring group for your job or your business, get down to a sports club, sing with a choir or start a fish lovers vegan knitting circle. It doesn't matter what it is, just get connecting with people. The subject matter doesn't matter. The people around you matter. It doesn't matter what you do, just deepen some relationships in your life. The benefit you have on the world will magnify exponentially. And be kind. That's all it takes.

For Results – Remember that your results do not determine your happiness; your happiness determines your results. Be really clear about the results you want and then take time to reflect on your achievements when you reach your goals. Don't move your goal posts or do it to other people. Happiness is not over the horizon of the next result. It's in the here and now – and it can be now.

For Expression – remember that emotions are what make us human. Learn to appreciate art, beauty and the world around you. Listen to people when they have something to share with you. Sing in the shower, have fun, learn salsa, pick up a paintbrush or a guitar or write a book or a poem. Appreciate the artistry of the people who bake or cook for you. Eat great food. It doesn't need to be expensive; it just needs to be created with love. A simple meal of bread and cheese can be exquisite if you take time to notice it. The key to a full life doesn't just lie in working harder. Enjoy music, it's one of the most powerful ways to anchor-in the memory of something exquisite.

For Discovery – Stay playful! Stay interested, and you will stay interesting. Look for patterns, connect dots, challenge yourself to learn and

---

[90.] That study has been going for over 75 years and has followed the lives of over 500 people.
[91.] View the TED talk about the study by Study Director Robert Waldinger at https://www.ted.com/talks/robert_waldinger_what_makes_a_good_life_lessons_from_the_longest_study_on_happiness/

discover new things. Be like Sister Bernadette. Try something you have never tried before at least every month. Ask lots of daft questions and remember that there's no such thing as a daft question.

Do those things and you will stay on fire and light the path for others to do the same. Do those things in your company and you will have a great place to work and be a great person to work for.

Pay It Forward

What we do and which flames light us up the most really are demonstrating just one thing. Who we are. Our very essence.

The actions we CHOOSE to take, reflect the very essence of who we are and what we believe in. They show the world what we value. The flames that illuminate us also serve to reflect the very core of our identity. The light and energy we bring to the world is essence of who we really are.

If there is a core message from this book it is not just about following your passion. It's discovering new flames that could give you new insights. It's about understanding who you really are, then using that knowledge to have more impact on other people. As Zig Ziglar said, "You can have everything *you* ever want if you help enough other people get what *they* want". The message of this book is to find your gifts, amplify them, do more with them and uncover new areas of potential that you might not have explored yet. If you do the same for other people; children, friends and colleagues then you will have shared that gift and who knows what you could unleash because of that ...

Many of the people I have been fortunate enough to connect with for this book have talked about the energy fields and hidden forces that shape our lives. Those forces shape our decisions and have massive effects on our own physiology and on the world around us. I believe that technology is just on the brink of bringing some concepts that have been around for along time into the mainstream. There are scientists who are starting to be able to measure our emotional energy and directly correlate those levels to our health and well-being. The leap forward in quantum technology and the effect of light on our cells is something that we are starting to be able to measure. So, the 5 flames is much more than a way to help you remember what fires people up and provide fuel for some fun conversations around the office (though I really hope you get to do that too ... 5 flames posters available for you to download with my compliments.)[92]

11.2 Clues to Your Purpose

You now understand the characteristics of the 5 flames, and I hope they have helped you start to make sense of why you love the things that you love, and why you can't stand some of the things that drive you nuts! I hope it helps you make sense of other people too.

I think some of the messages that pop up all over the Internet about 'living the dream' and finding 'your passion' and 'living your purpose' might be inspirational but lead many people to feel discontent. After all, the people who seem to have the time to post pictures of their lovely houses, Instagram every aspect of their beautiful lives and post filtered images of their perfect happy children could make anyone question why they are having to deal with crap in their lives. At some point we will all be dogged by worries about getting a job, starting a business, dealing with an unhappy boss, not making the sales figures, nursing sick kids, caring for ageing parents or the million and one other things that make everyone's real lives much less glamorous than we might dream about. It's far more realistic to accept what you can't change and learn how to change your reactions to things. OK, so you might not love every element of what you do in your job or your business. So what? None of us lives inside Instagram or a Facebook advert and make a million in 10 weeks with no effort. We live in the real world. We have problems. We don't feel great all the time. And you know what; it's OK. It's life. It's how it is. It doesn't make you unsuccessful. It makes you

---

[92.] www.sophiebennett.com/resources

human. People won't remember you for what you've done, they'll remember you for what you've overcome.

Now here's the upside. As you go through all these things, you learn about yourself. Every time you get a knock back you learn how to treat other people better and every-time someone is nice to you, you become a nicer person to other people afterwards. Being kind is catching, and you don't need a big bank balance or to run the company to be nice to people. It's one thing to be motivated, it's something else to be so focused on a goal to the point where you forget what's important.

There is a reason why the inclusion section of this book is bigger than the rest of the flame sections. It's because it's the people in our companies, our families and our social circles that make us happier, healthier and better off.

Use the idea of the five flames to make your life fuller and to help you pay attention to those little moments that lift your heart. Those little moments give you clues that you can pay attention to. At some point in the future, you will be looking for something new to do. Maybe you will want to get a new job, try a new challenge or start a business. File those heart-lifting moments away because they are the key to you getting clearer about what fires you up, so you can spend more time doing what you love to do as you move through life.

Maybe you have had a revelation or two reading this book. Maybe you realised that your most enjoyable moments are solitary and that you really love being in flow. Maybe you understood that Inclusion is the key to what makes you happy and all your dreams have other people in them. Maybe you have finally acknowledged that you get off on results and that you need to complete, to win or to see a score before you are happy. Winning is great, and it's a habit worth cultivating. Maybe you have finally admitted you have an artistic side and you want to throw caution to the wind and open a craft bakery in a hick village somewhere in the borderlands, or maybe you've realised that you never feel satisfied unless you are learning something. Then best of luck in your quest for scientific, comic, human or spiritual enlightenment.

I hope you have clues that could lead you to a better job, a business you can relish, a group of friends who share your passions and a new understanding of the power of relationships.

Whatever you get out of this book I trust you will share your motivation with others and help them see what lights them up too. If you are in a leadership position, then you have the opportunity to set an example to others by living a great life and doing a great job.

What you do matters.

How you look after yourself and nourish your passion matters.

How you treat other people matters.

How do you express yourself and listen to others do the same, really matters.

Pushing the boundaries of what's humanly possible matters.

I've always wondered how many virtuoso violin players there are out there who have never picked up a violin? How many potential record-breaking athletes there are who've never been timed running or jumped a high bar? How many gifted writers are there who have never read a book from cover to cover? How many poets who have never dared to write down their words? We all matter. Our passions **matter**. We are all motivated by something but if we don't pay attention to the moments that matter, we could miss our greatest calling.

If you want to take increasing control of your life, your career, your success and what you love to do, it's up to you to start using the flames to make your life better.

- Use the idea of Flow to pay attention to the things that suspend time for you and that make you feel balanced, focused and at one with the world.
- Use the idea of Inclusion to bring others along with you, to be the positive energy that other people want to be around and to create a buzz that makes everyone feel better, including yourself.
- Use the idea of Results to keep making progress and to learn to take responsibility for your life. Results help you see how far

you've come, plan where you are going next and measure your progress.

- Use the idea of Expression to stay in touch with your artistic and emotional side. As you build more and more of the material side of your life, it will be this that adds depth and meaning to your life.

- And finally, use the idea of Discovery to stay curious. It's your curiosity to learn new things that always opens the possibilities of finding an element of your role that you didn't know existed, seeing the opportunities of a new business or product idea, igniting a new passion, hobby or friendship. Our curiosity is one of the greatest gifts that we have.

I'm going to finish on an excerpt from a commencement speech Steve Jobs, the late co-founder of Apple and Pixar Studios gave at Stanford University. It was 2005, a year after he was diagnosed with pancreatic cancer and just over 6 years before he was to leave us.

Steve Jobs found his flame. He left his mark on the planet. Now it's your turn.

> *"Your work is going to fill a large part of your life, and the only way to be truly satisfied is to do what you believe is great work. And the only way to do great work is to love what you do. If you haven't found it yet, keep looking. Don't settle. As with all matters of the heart, you'll know when you find it. And, like any great relationship, it just gets better and better as the years roll on. So keep looking until you find it . . .*
> *. . . have the courage to follow your heart and intuition. They somehow already know what you truly want to become. Everything else is secondary."*

> **Steve Jobs**

PART 3
Beyond The Book

Finding Your Flame

Are you still looking for your flame? Are you are considering a career change, or stepping up the leadership ladder?

Planning a life shift? Thinking of starting a new venture? Are you a point in your life where you aren't sure where to focus your efforts?

Then it's probably the perfect time for you to Find your Flame.

Maybe it's time for you to rekindle some of the things you once loved, or maybe it's time to find new flames that will ignite you and lift your spirit.

I'm passionate about helping people find their flame, start living a life that they love and doing work they really care about. Check out my website to get the resources you need to ignite your life and work.

Achievers International

I also have a company that helps corporate clients to bring the 5 Flames philosophy into companies and runs public programs to help individuals find their flames and turn them into sustainable ventures. I co-founded Achievers International with author and entrepreneur Warren Cass to help you succeed. We are RESULTS motivated and it's YOUR RESULTS we care about.

Warren and I, together with our team of world class experts deliver seminars, mastermind sessions and workshops that help you thrive in a knowledge economy. To find out about what it takes to be an International Achiever and to discover what we are running in your area, visit us at www.achievers-international.com.

If you loved this book and want to make sure you stay in the loop about my future books, visit www.sophiebennett.com, sign up to the newsletter and get further resources to help you and your team ignite!

Keynotes and Speaking

You can hire Sophie Bennett as an inspirational speaker for your next event. The *Find Your Flame* Keynote takes the audience on a journey of discovery about what really motivates them, and gives insights into how you can inspire others in innovative ways. Sophie's talks are designed with care and delivered with a passion so people can light up their own lives and lift the spirit of their teams and organisations.

The presentation can also be adapted to meet the unique needs of your audience. Other talks are available on request. Sophie speaks in the UK, Europe, and the USA and hopes to be visiting Asia to speak in the near future.

To find out more, discover other presentation topics Sophie offers and watch a video her speaking from stage, visit:

www.sophiebennett.com/keynote.

That's also the place to make an enquiry about availability or to get in touch with Sophie to discuss the needs for your conference or event.

Media

Sophie is an experienced interview guest. She has appeared on the radio, is an enthusiastic podcast guest, and is comfortable both on video and in front of the camera. For enquiries and interviews, get in touch via her website or reach out to her directly and connect on LinkedIn at www.linkedin/in/sophiebennettUK.

As a committed writer, she is always happy to provide articles for publication on websites, blogs, and magazines.

Fired Up Leadership

It's all very well discovering new things about successful people and turning those ideas into something that we can hopefully learn from. The next step is to work out how we can turn that learning into successful outcomes.

Each of the flames has a skillset attached to it; skills that come naturally to someone who has that particular flame in abundance. When it's our secondary flame, it's an easy win development opportunity. For our less bright flames, these are areas and skills where we could probably see the biggest wins and the most rapid improvements in performance and personal effectiveness.

For each flame, there is an action that comes from it. That's what we help people to develop as part of Fired Up Leadership Programmes.

Developed in Collaboration with Dr Jacquie Drake PhD MBA

Dr Jacquie Drake[93] has been pivotal in helping me to turn the five flames of motivation into actionable learning and development that you can access for your organisation. Each programme consists of a series of modules meticulously designed to help leaders, future leaders and organisations tap into natural motivational patterns and lift leadership skills to new heights. We are here to help people get focused, ready to lead, be accountable, communicate effectively and to innovate for the future.

Here's what our programmes help people to do:

Get into Flow and develop focus. Where there is no focus, there is no flow – and where there is no flow, mastery will always be elusive. If you want to become *really* good at anything, learning what it takes to get into flow is an essential skill. Flow-motivated people will do that naturally, but most of us won't and we need to learn how.

---

[93] Jacquie has 35 years' experience in developing leaders at all levels and has a track record of success in pioneering radical new approaches to leadership development at top global business schools and in blue-chip organisations.
She works both as a consultant and executive coach and is also currently lecturing on MBA, MSc and Executive programmes at Cranfield School of Management, the Defence Academy, Mannheim Business School, the Cyprus International Institute of Management, and Euromoney, London & Hong Kong. Her specialisms are: leadership, communication, team dynamics, personal development, performance management and organisational change.

Create Inclusion and build leadership capability. It's about working out how to be a part of an effective team and what an effective team sounds, looks and feels like. How do you bring in people from the margins? How do you get a diverse group of people to work as a crack-team who deliver beyond expectations? Inclusion-motivated people will do that naturally, but most of us won't and we need to learn how.

Deliver Results by getting accountable. Without the confidence to be responsible, results will be coincidental at best and delivery will be patchy. It takes personal responsibility, courage and resilience to be fully accountable and consistently deliver results. Results-motivated people will do this naturally, but most of us won't and we need to learn how.

Enhance Expression through great communication. It's not always easy when our emotions interfere with our clarity of thinking. It's not easy to be honest and express ourselves eloquently. It's a key skill to learn and keep developing through the course of our careers. Expression-motivated people do that naturally, but most of us won't and we need to learn how.

Discover and innovate through increasing curiosity. It takes courage to be innovative and that can be a challenge when we still have the day job to do. Many of us are searching for great questions and tools to stay curious, creative, alive and fresh. Discovery-motivated people do that naturally, but most of us won't and we need to learn how.

For more information about the Fired Up Leadership programs visit www.sophiebennett.com/leadership.

About the Author

Sophie Bennett is an inspiring keynote speaker and the author of several books. Her first book **Money Bondage** – *Discover the Power of Mind Over Money* is a personal development and finance book that focuses on our behaviours and beliefs around money. It reached the top of the Amazon charts and stayed there for several months, was featured in the national media and was well received by critics and readers alike.

Formerly a high-performance equestrian athlete (a horsewoman and a skier) Sophie has an endless fascination with what motivates people to do extraordinary things and has spent over 30 years studying the science of high achievement.

She is now a successful speaker, runs a successful leadership consultancy and continues to write daily. Her business books have been nominated for several awards.

Sophie is married and lives in Gloucestershire, England surrounded by books, dogs, horses, and treasured friends.

You can connect with her at
www.linkedin.com/in/sophiebennettuk
www.facebook.com/sophiebennettUK
Twitter @sophiebennettUK
email pa@sophiebennett.com

Acknowledgements

Fifty driven and inspiring people were gracious enough to be interviewed for this book and without them it would have been a one-dimensional piece of work. Every one of them was a springboard for ideas that led to some very interesting places. They are the stars of this book. Every interview revealed a new insight on what it takes to be successful and what it means to do it with integrity. Thank you.

Special thanks to Stuart Crainer, Co-founder of Thinkers50 for writing the Foreword. I'm humbled.

Suzy Walker, editor of Psychologies gave her perspective on the main idea and helped more than I can say on one page. Brian Tracy, who knows the value of his personal brand, put his weight behind the project and his involvement opened many doors; thank you Brian. Dorie Clark's advice sharpened my previously bumbling interview technique and her style and content continues to influence my work. Robert Craven convinced me that it was a project worth starting and was unwavering in his determination to keep me accountable. His no-nonsense support has been my secret productivity weapon and I'm lucky to have had his wisdom guiding me. Christian Kromme's clarity and optimism about the need for the book kept my enthusiasm high when the work got gritty.

Thanks go to Peter Saxton, Jacquie Drake, Warren Cass, Stephanie Hale, Barnaby Wynter, for bouncing ideas, cover concepts, reading drafts and various contributions that moved the book forward and to my skiing buddies Simon, Chris and Dave for pushing me over the finish line. Nienke Van Bezooijen is an ace advisor on turning a book into a speech, Sue Richardson was a voice of common sense over the final title, and Henk Bremer's insight and experience on the leadership needs of global corporations helped shape some of the early ideas. Jason Anscomb did a great job of the cover design.

The team at home always have a lot to put up with when I have a book project I really care about in full swing. Heaven help them. Appreciation to my husband Henry who fielded life while I was immersed until silly o'clock for months on end, to Tracey Preater who knows how to keep me organised, to Allen, and to Sanah Vij (I wish I could have employed you!). Thanks to Miles, Rachel and Adrian at Choir Press for taking the manuscript and turning it into a book.

I also wish to express gratitude to the hundreds of people who contributed to the survey; your generosity and feedback provided many new insights that proved to be invaluable. With every book there are always people who have had an impact who didn't make the acknowledgement page due to my shocking memory and poor note taking. The fault is all mine and the kindness all yours.

Lightning Source UK Ltd.
Milton Keynes UK
UKHW01f0648021018
329873UK00011B/631/P